IN THIS
Moment

IN THIS
Moment

JACQUELINE SHAKESPEARE

The working mother's
guide to a calm and
fulfilling life

What working mothers are saying about *In This Moment*

'This is an engaging, inspiring and wonderfully practical read. Jacqueline speaks so much common sense – I found myself agreeing with everything she said and wondering why I hadn't worked it out for myself before. A great book that will help all us working mothers keep sorted, satisfied and sane.'

— **Joanna Courtney,** mother to Hannah and Alec, stepmother to Emily and Rory, Author of the *Queens of the Conquest* series

'Being a working mum requires constant juggling, but this candid, practical book will help professional mothers keep those balls in the air. What's more, Jacqueline's inspirational story of her own journey to contentment shows that it's OK to drop the balls from time to time. Perfection isn't the goal – it's about achieving a happy balance between family and career and enjoying every moment of the performance.'

— **Anne Marie Ryan,** mother to Eve and Rose, writer and editor

'A great compact guide to help with working mothers' everyday lives. Jacqueline's book really hits the spot when it comes to kind, practical guidance on how to live a less stressed and more contented life as a working mother. I particularly valued the advice on how to slow down and live more in the moment, which I am now applying religiously to my own weekends. Jacqueline's personal stories on how she became a more balanced and contented mother will keep you engaged as you absorb the more pragmatic suggestions alongside.'

   — **Anna Wood,** mother to Lilah and Johnny, Senior University Manager

'Being a working mum is often really hard so it's great to receive such good advice and support from someone who's been there. In this book Jacqueline offers up her experience and wisdom in such a practical, yet kind, friendly, honest and open manner that it's like sitting down with a friend whose shoulder you know you can lean on. Her experiences will resonate with a lot of women while also making them feel saner and calmer. Easily digestible and packed with tried and tested methods for restoring balance, this book is a godsend for busy mums.'

   — **Beth Gregory,** mother to Izzy and James, Marketing and Communications Manager

'As I'm a mother who questions her every decision, this book made me clearly see that it's OK not to be perfect. A great read where I often found myself becoming accepting of my career choices, both as a mother and as an executive in my field. Filled with useful tips and invaluable tools, Jacqueline's book makes a working mother's life that bit easier.'

— **Dina Polydorou,** mother to Erini and Dimitri, Senior Associate in Executive Search

'If you are trying to balance your career and personal responsibilities, or find yourself at a crossroads in your professional life, then read this book. Jacqueline has shared her personal experiences as a working mother in an open and honest account, and recommends a fantastic set of tools to help manage our busy lives. An inspiring read that will motivate and guide you to make positive changes for you, your career and your family.'

— **Adèle Phelan,** mother to Orla and Daniel, Speech Therapist

'This book provides practical advice on getting the balance right for yourself and your family. The personal experiences which Jacqueline shares throughout the book really resonated with me and reassured me that I should feel proud to be a working mum, that it's OK to ask for help, and I can be safe in the knowledge that my working is likely to have a positive rather than negative impact on my children. This book has something to offer working mothers everywhere.'

— **Louise Beiteverde,** mother to Emilia and Jonathan, Respiratory Nurse

'Working mums everywhere will find lots of great hints and tips in Jacqueline's book. Her story reflects our lives too, and she's not afraid to be open and honest about the fact that we don't need to be perfect. What we should be aiming for is to be good enough and to focus on what really matters.'

— **Gabriella Evans,** mother to Thomas and Joshua, Chartered Accountant

RETHINK PRESS

First published in Great Britain in 2019 by Rethink Press
(www.rethinkpress.com)

© Copyright Jacqueline Shakespeare

For my daughter, whose first ambition was to be a part-time teacher, a doctor and a fairy. You can achieve everything you want to in life, my darling.

And for my son. Keep dancing and laughing, sweet boy, you bring so much joy to the world.

Contented *(adjective)*
'In a state of peaceful happiness'.

I believe in being contented.

When we measure the success of our lives on how much time we spend being filled with euphoric happiness, we are misleading ourselves into thinking that these temporary happy moments are how we're always supposed to feel. When the moment of pure joy passes, it feels like a loss. This triggers us to seek more feelings of happiness in a never-ending cycle.

When we strive for contentment as working mothers, we free ourselves to appreciate where we are in the whole of our lives rather than oscillating between moments of happiness back to our natural state of being. We accept and embrace the highs and lows of life in peaceful contentment.

Contents

Introduction

Sugar and spice and all things nice

Once upon a time, when we were young, we dreamt about our lives when we grew up. We wanted to be ballerinas, police officers and teachers, train drivers, mothers and artists. Anything was possible in our dreams.

We didn't see any reason why we couldn't pursue more than one of these at a time. It's not that we were overly ambitious, we just never imagined we couldn't have everything we wanted. We worked hard at school, focused on building our careers, steadily learning and achieving more and more. Our lives were full of exciting discoveries, parties with friends, Sunday lunches with family.

Then we had children. Our wonderful bundles of joy who light up our days and our lives. The only thing is, having a career and being a mother feels so much harder than we ever expected it to. Instead of a balanced and harmonious life, we feel like we spend much of our time muddling through and we start to question whether it's really possible to have a fulfilling career while still being the mother that our children need us to be.

Somewhere inside all of us are those little girls who started off believing we could have everything we wanted and are now facing the reality of those dreams.

Life doesn't come with instructions

Take a pen and make a note of any of the following that resonate:

- I'm worried I'm not there for my kids when they need me

- I let guilt influence my behaviour and actions

- Everything is down to me in the home – without me on top of everything, birthdays would be forgotten, packed lunches wouldn't be made, it would all fall apart

- I feel like I never get any time for me

- I compare myself to people who have made different life choices

- I try to do everything myself

- I don't think I can pursue my career and still be the person I want to be on a personal level

- I don't even try to have a meaningful career because it feels completely unattainable

- I feel like I need to apologise for being a mother when I'm at work

- I'm not challenged fully at work; I don't use all the skills and experiences I have developed over my career

- I don't go for interesting opportunities or promotions at work because I assume I won't be successful

- I don't feel I can change jobs because I can't risk what I have today in terms of flexibility

- I feel like I haven't got a clue most of the time; that I'm faking it and I'm just waiting to get caught out

- I feel exhausted

If just one of these statements resonates with you, then this book will help.

In our professional lives, we go on courses when we are learning a new skill, or we shadow a colleague. We may have mentors or coaches who help us along the way. In a supportive, professional environment, we are given the help we need to make sure we are successful.

When we have children, we are guided by family members and other parents. We may join groups with other new mothers, and together with our children, we find our way. When we go back to work, though, we face one of the most challenging times of our lives. Although we may have friends in the same position, and the ongoing support of family and those around us, the challenges we each face are complex and tough.

We find ourselves fumbling our way through our days, pleading with our children to put their shoes on before we're late for school. A long day of back-to-back appointments where we barely have time to go to the loo or eat, and an evening of tidying up, feeding the family and trying to prepare for the next day. Thoughts of how there must be an easier way flash through our heads before we crash out, then it all starts again in the morning.

We feel overwhelmed, knowing that we've taken on more than is feasible for one human being. We're exhausted and wracked with guilt for not spending enough time with our children. A friend sees how frazzled we are and suggests we take up Pilates. Of course we should, but when on earth are we supposed to fit it in?

Being a working mother is tough. Really tough. The pressure in today's society on mothers who choose or need to work is enormous. The pressure we put on ourselves is enormous. We are expected to be everything to everyone. The perfect mother, at school pick up each day and at every form assembly, while at the same time demonstrating our full commitment at work. It can be overwhelming and many mothers feel they can't pursue a fulfilling career without it compromising the other areas of their lives.

We crave guidance and an understanding of how to best navigate our way through. There are no magic wands and fairy dust that will make everything feel easy, but there is a simple path to reach contentment in your life, and it's easier to follow than you may think.

Knowing the rules of the game

My family have always enjoyed playing games together. A few years ago, I bought Monopoly Deal, a card game where the aim is to be the first person to build three property sets. It involves a bit of luck in terms of the cards you are dealt, but then it's about how you play the game.

The four of us played a few times. My husband, son and I were really enjoying it, but my daughter quickly became frustrated; she wasn't winning any of the games. Later that evening, I went into her room to find her sitting on the floor, the rules on one side of her and the cards on the other. She was playing against herself over and over again, improving by becoming more familiar with the rules and through experience of playing the game. Each time she played, she was learning and refining her skills. The next day, she was desperate to play us all, and lo and behold, she won quite a few of the games.

Being a contented working mother is a lot like a game of Monopoly Deal. You need to know the rules and then you need to practise. The rules aren't complex; the hard part is the practice and willingness to learn from your mistakes. By doing this, you minimise the tough days and find the contentment in your lives that you want.

I have two children, and apart from my maternity leaves, I have always worked – part time, full time, in jobs I've loved and in some I've hated. I am now a partner in a London-based consultancy firm – we help clients solve complex business problems. It's hard work – we're building a business, so that's inevitable – but there's a lot of energy and fun in our team. I love it.

At times, like every other working mother, I've felt exhausted with the reality of just making it through the day. Weary from the constant demands on me, the never-ending juggling. I've had days, and sometimes weeks, where it feels unbearably tough. At my lowest points, I have been known to sink to the kitchen floor at the end of the working day with a glass of wine in my hand, numb with guilt, convinced I had my priorities all wrong.

But I'm determined to enjoy my life and to be a contented mother. So over the last fourteen years, since my daughter was born, I have learned the rules of the game and identified the five principles and five skills that are consistently demonstrated by contented working mothers. I have tried and tested these principles and skills over and over and I know they work. I don't manage to follow them perfectly every day, and in the middle of a tough day, I often wish I was better at following my own advice, but when I do follow them, I know that I'm calmer and more contented.

I hope that the principles and skills in this book will help you too. When you learn them and practise and experiment with them, they will help you to stop feeling as though you are muddling your way through each day. Instead, you can breathe more deeply, smile and be proud of what you are achieving. You can find joy in your life as a contented working mother and have a fulfilling career without having to compromise other areas of your life.

How to use the book

The book is in four parts.

Part 1 reviews the impact on our children when we work, and the reality of what is making it all feel so hard.

Part 2 looks at the five principles that help you to be your best mental and physical self, ready to face all of the tough challenges working mothers have to deal with every day.

Part 3 looks at the five skills demonstrated by contented working mothers. These skills are practical and require an organised approach, which will sit more easily with some of you than others. But whatever your predisposition towards some strong structure in your life, it's important to persist with them. Without a certain level of control around your day to day, you will struggle to ever be a contented working mother.

Once you are equipped with the working mother principles and skills, Part 4 looks at how you continue on your journey to being a contented working mother.

PART ONE
IN THE BEGINNING

1
This Woman's Work, This Woman's World

'Your story is what you have, what you will always have. It is something to own.'
— Michelle Obama, *Becoming*

Women have always worked outside the home and there have always been challenges. It's easy to imagine those we face today are more testing than at any other time in history, but they aren't; they're just different.

Seventy years ago, when my paternal grandmother married, she was forced to give up work under the custom and practice of the marriage bar. The bar was in place because it was believed that women who were married didn't need jobs as they would be supported by their husbands, and that unmarried women were more reliable and mobile than married women.

This practice seems inconceivable in today's society and the marriage bar has been lifted. The World Wars helped to demonstrate how women could take men's traditional places in factories and contribute to the economy alongside men. The number of mothers (and women in general) in work steadily rose over the course of the last century until, by the 1980s, over half of mothers in the UK were working.

Now in almost three-quarters of families with dependent children, the women – 4.9 million of us – are working either part time or full time.[1] The number of mothers with dependent children employed in England has risen by more than a million since records began in 1996.

In parallel, the length of the average working day has increased. Twenty years ago, it was around seven hours, and now it has increased by about two hours. But the needs of our children and the structure of childcare has barely changed. Mothers with school-age children juggle their working hours as well as they can alongside afterschool clubs, childminders and nannies in term time. During the holidays, they deplete hard-earned funds and use up precious holiday entitlement trying to cover the days where

---

1   Office for National Statistics www.ons.gov.uk, 'Families and the Labour Market, England: 2017'

there is no childcare on hand. The Utopia of flexible working is often just the ability to leave the office at 5pm, rush to collect the children and go through the evening family routine before picking up work and starting again once the children are in bed.

And finally, the dynamic inside the home is changing. Lifelong marriages between two people of the opposite sex are on the decline, and so is the traditional nuclear family with a mother, father and their biological children. There is a diversity in our homes that we have never seen before, with single parents, same-sex relationships, stepchildren, foster children and adopted children.

There will always be external factors influencing how we work and the environments we work in, and no doubt the dynamics within our industries and our homes will always evolve and mature. As working women, we need to continue to challenge ourselves and our environments, be flexible and adaptable, and keep trying out new ways to make it work for us.

The choices we make

We all make individual and personal choices on whether we return to work after having children.

For many women, working is essential if we are to pay the mortgage or maintain the lifestyles we have become accustomed to, or want, for our growing families. In many families, this cannot be achieved on one salary alone. Property prices and the cost of living have soared over the last twenty years; our hard-earned money simply doesn't go as far as it once did. At the same time, many of us want and expect experiences and material goods that in the past, only the wealthier could enjoy: the latest gadgets, monthly subscriptions to stream music and foreign holidays. All this comes at a price and puts pressure on the family income.

Some mothers choose to work for the sense of purpose it gives to them. They have worked hard all their lives to build their career and they don't see why they need to give it up just because they have children.

When my first child was born, my daughter, I returned to work after six months, full time. It was incredibly hard leaving her at such a young age, even though I knew she was with a caring childminder. On many occasions, I had to fight back the tears as I left her. Only when I reached the safety of my car did I allow myself to have a little weep.

I applied for part-time working numerous times, but I was repeatedly turned down on the grounds that the organisation didn't believe it was possible to do my job in fewer than five days a week. My full-time salary enabled us to move from a small London flat into a house large enough for a second child; a home we could see ourselves settling in for many years. From a financial perspective, it all made sense, but I never got used to leaving my daughter in the arms of someone else, even though I knew she was happy. I found it really tough.

My son was born two and a half years after my daughter. This time, a new opportunity arose while I was on maternity leave: I was offered a job which could be done on a part-time basis. I jumped at the offer and returned to work three days a week.

Like many working mothers, I never felt my life was going perfectly, but I found my way through. When my son was eight, I ended up in a position where I was under more stress at work than I was able to cope with and I knew that the situation wasn't going to change. I therefore made the decision to leave my permanent job and work for myself as an independent consultant. Although it meant stepping away from being part time, it was the right decision for me and my family. A happy mother working full time is far better than a deeply unhappy part-time one.

If I'm honest with myself, it was easy for me to 'blame' financial reasons for my return to work. That was the main driver, but it allowed me to avoid having to make a far more difficult emotional decision. I've always enjoyed working (when I'm in the right job), and on reflection, I would have missed the richness and breadth my career gives me had I stopped working.

I'll never make it on to the board of a FTSE-100 company (nor do I want to), I don't make it to World Book Day assembly, and the door handle on my lounge door fell off about two years ago and we haven't got around to fixing it yet. But we're doing OK. We have messy days where everything seems to fall apart, we shout sometimes, along with every other family in the country, but we also laugh and we dance and we enjoy life.

The whole of us

Richard Ackoff was an organisational theorist and a pioneer in the field of systems thinking. A system consists of elements, interconnections and a purpose, and we are all members of numerous systems. A sports team is a system, with elements such as players, a coach, field and a ball. Interconnections are the rules of the game, the strategies and communication between the players. The purpose is to win games, exercise and have fun.

Systems thinking focuses on the way a system's constituent parts interrelate and how over time they work within larger systems. If we think of our lives as a system, we need to consider how our professional and our homes lives interrelate. However much we want to, we can never truly separate them. We may be trying to leave work on time on Tuesday because it's our child's first day in Year 5, or leaving home early in the morning before the children are awake so that we can get into work and prepare for an important meeting. The different areas of our lives will always bump into each other and sometimes conflict.

We shouldn't try and manage each part of our lives in isolation, determined to be the best we can be in each area as if it didn't connect with anything else. Striving to be the star employee will probably involve more sacrifices than we are prepared to make at home. We no longer have the same hours in the day to dedicate to our career as we did before we had children. In turn, being a great mother cannot be defined by whether we turn up to every sports day, harvest festival and school pick up. When we focus too heavily on one area of our lives and it dominates, it is at the detriment of the other parts of our lives. We end up feeling like the different areas of our lives are in conflict.

The key is to nurture and care for each area of our lives, but understand how to be our best whole. Each individual area can give us so much, but we need to maintain perspective and remember what we are trying to achieve overall.

You can be the mother you want to be and have a fulfilling professional journey. But you need to redefine what success is to you now you have children and look across your whole life for overall contentment. Being a contented working mother isn't about having a magazine-shoot-ready home at the same time as being the CEO of a multinational corporation who manages to find time to be at every school event and heads off to a spa weekend once a month. In reality, most of us are just working to get to the end of the month and pay the bills. It's about having happy children who get all the love and support they need from us. It's about having a slightly messy home that we love; a career which isn't necessarily high flying, but fulfils and stretches us. Oh, and a bit of me time occasionally as well.

2
In Data We Trust

'Without data you're just another person with an opinion.'
   — W. Edwards Deming

We often see, hear and feel the prejudices, opinions and pressures from society for us to be at home for our children. But when we look at the data, are we really compromising our relationship with our children and their future happiness when we work?

We want our children to be happy and to grow into well-balanced and successful adults. It's recognised that one-to-one time with children is critical for their cognitive, behavioural and academic development. Strong relationships are key; what's less important is whether these relationships are with a parent or other caring adults, including members of the family and childminders. In fact, there are huge benefits to a child's development when they forge strong relationships with people outside the immediate family circle.

Being a role model as a working mother, we set our children up for future success. A major study was conducted by Harvard University, published in 2015[2] and led by Harvard Business School professor Kathleen McGinn. This study shows clearly that the daughters of working mothers enjoy better careers, higher pay and more equal relationships than those raised by stay-at-home mothers. Sons of working mothers were shown to spend more time contributing to household chores and caring for family members.

McGinn points in her study to the guilt that parents feel about both of them working outside the home, and that there's no need for them to feel this way. Her research clearly shows that working parents not only help their families economically, they also help themselves professionally and emotionally (if they love their jobs) and help their kids.

---

2   'Kids of Working Moms Grow into Happy Adults', HBS, Kathleen L. McGinn, 2018

The study concluded that:

> '... there are very few things... that have such a clear effect on gender inequality as being raised by a working mother. In short, it's good for your kids.'

And finally, when we look at our need to spend time with our children for our own wellbeing and happiness, we can comfort ourselves in the knowledge that as mothers, we are actually spending more time with our children than our parents did with us, irrespective of whether we work or not. In 1965, mothers spent an average of 54 minutes each day with their children, while mothers in 2012 averaged almost twice that at 104 minutes per day.[3] Fathers' time with children over the same period nearly quadrupled. On average today, fathers spend fifty-nine minutes each day with their children.

Interestingly, a friend once commented that I spent more quality time with my children than she did, even though she wasn't working and I was. Her observation was based around the fact that when I was at home, I was focusing on my children, whereas when her children returned home from school, they went off to play in the garden or watch television while she continued with her household jobs.

---

3   'Educational Gradients in Parents' Child-Care Time Across Countries, 1965–2012', Giulia M Dotti Sani and Judith Treas, Journal of Marriage and Family, 2016

It's hard for some of us to hear that the main role in our child's development doesn't have to be taken on by us for it to be most beneficial. It's hard for us to be away from our children on an emotional level, but we need to remember we are spending more time with them than mothers in previous generations. The data confirms that being a working mother is good for us, it's good for our daughters and good for our sons. We can feel comfortable working and knowing that we are not compromising our children's future happiness and success.

What's making this feel so hard?

Working mothers face tough challenges every single day. There are three main ones that work against us: society's perceptions of working mothers, that we live in a complex world, and the inequality in the home.

Society's perceptions of working mothers. Mothers have always worked. The difference between now and a few decades ago is firstly that we are stepping into careers that historically were dominated by men, and secondly, we are often working for our own sense of purpose as well as for financial gain.

Although there are many individuals and parts of society that fully support working mothers on an emotional and practical level, there are also many areas where views on working mothers have not kept pace with the rate of change. As a result, working mothers today still face judgment, prejudice and push back. There are many people who still firmly believe that a mother's place is in the home.

In the USA, 51% of adults believe children are better off if the mother is at home and not working,[4] while only 34% said children are just as well off if their mother works. What makes this statistic worse is when it's compared against views on fathers working outside the home: 76% of American adults felt that children are just as well off if their father works.

In a study based in the UK, The Fawcett Society[5] found that 60% of people, both men and women, believe a man's commitment to his job isn't affected when he becomes a father; 11% believe they are less committed, but nearly 29% think men are more committed to their job after becoming a father. For women, it is a different story. While 47% believe that when a woman has a child her commitment to her job is not affected, just 8% think she is more committed, and a huge 46% believe a woman becomes less committed to her job after having children.

No matter how robust our beliefs in our own ability to be great working mothers, it's tough to face into such

---

4   Pew Research Center, 'Breadwinner Moms', May 2013
5   'Parents, Work and Care: Striking the balance', Jemima Olchawski, The Fawcett Society, 2016

deep-rooted opinions as these every day. They make the most confident of us question our choices.

We live in a complex world. Humans are most comfortable living in a world where a specific action causes a predictable outcome – a simple environment. We run and become fitter. We read books on a chosen subject and become more knowledgeable. We can easily understand this straightforward environment and can operate in it without difficulty.

But the world isn't always that simple and predictable. Sometimes we experience complicated situations where knowledge alone isn't enough to predict the outcome. We need to draw on our instinct to help. This is the world of surgeons, architects, criminologists and midwives. People who need the foundation of knowledge, but also use their experience and instinct to help them be the best they can be in their jobs.

Humans comfortably operate in both of these environments. They make sense to our rational selves and we broadly understand them. As mothers, much of our world sits within one of these two environments. We read to our children and their language skills develop; they fall over and we know how to comfort them.

However, our overall environment isn't one where there is a simple or even complicated relationship between our actions and our outcomes. It's complex.[6] This is an environment where cause and effect can only be deduced in retrospect; using our knowledge and instinct alone is no longer enough. Our children are constantly growing, maturing and having different needs. What worked last week with them may not work this week. One of our parents may become ill and we need to spend more time with them; our partner may secure a new job and isn't at home as much. We can never truly create stability as a mother; as soon as we feel like we're getting it right, something changes and alters everything again.

This is why being a mother feels so hard to get right... and keep it there.

It's a natural human tendency to try and manage our overall environment as though it were a simple or complicated one – the environments we understand and feel more comfortable operating in. We pull on our knowledge, instinct and experience. We try harder, but don't get the outcome we would expect, and we struggle to understand why when it's simply because our overall environment is a complex one.

To survive, we must have solid foundations in place – our principles and skills. Then we must always be ready to respond to change; experimentation is key. We need to be constantly harnessing different ideas, testing them out, finding out what works at that moment.

---

6   The Stacey Matrix, developed by Ralph D. Stacey

Inequality in the home. We frequently hear about the focus on driving equality in the workplace, yet equality in the home is really stuck.

Many a mother gets home from work after a long day, walks straight into the kitchen and begins to make the dinner. She washes up, tidies up, gets the children's sports kit ready for the next day, puts a quick wash on and gets the children ready for bed.

'Can I help?' her partner asks.

She rolls her eyes. 'No thanks, I've done everything now.'

Her weekends are filled with helping the children with homework, arranging presents for a party her child is going to next week, paying the bills that have come through that week.

Sound familiar?

In homes with opposite-sex partners, women still spend a greater proportion of their time on household chores than men[7] and have less leisure time. In developed countries, employed women in two-parent opposite-sex households report that they devote an average of 17.7 hours per week to caring for family members. Employed men reportedly devote about 9 hours per week. At the same time, women report

---

7   'Leisure Time in the UK: 2015', Office for National Statistics

spending an average of 17.8 hours per week on housework, while men report an average of 8.8 hours.[8]

Too often women, even those of us working full time, assume the lion's share of responsibilities in the home. We take on the managerial role while men pick and choose how they contribute. We've seen our mothers and grandmothers take on this role, so we are following the example we were set as we were growing up. We fear that blame for any failure will fall at our feet so daren't let any of it go.

Even when the 'jobs' are split evenly, there is the mental load women invariably take on. This is the invisible work: the organisation, planning and thinking we do to manage our lives and those of people dependent on us. Remembering to return the school trip form; gathering all the PE kits for the week; remembering family birthdays. It's often unsatisfying work that can feel incessant, relentless and exhausting.

If she is in a partnership, a working mother doesn't want 'help'; she wants and needs a partner who takes equal responsibility for the running of the home. A true partner has an emotional commitment to their home; they are not just someone who follows direction. They want the best for us and our career. When there are two of us working and we women are the ones taking on responsibility for running the home, it impacts on

---

8   'Children Benefit From Having a Working Mom', HBS, Kathleen L. McGinn, 2015

our wellbeing, the amount of time we have to spend with our children and on ourselves, and also on our ability to succeed in our career.

It doesn't have to be this way. In Part 2, we will take a detailed look at my principles for living a contented life as a working mother.

PART TWO
THE WORKING MOTHER'S PRINCIPLES

3

Principle One – Know That Good Is Good Enough

'*Le mieux est l'ennemi du bien.*'
(The perfect is the enemy of the good.)
— Voltaire

Before we had children, it was relatively easy to find time to satisfy each area of our lives, whether that was relaxing with our partners and friends, focusing our energy on developing our careers, or 'me time'. We could comfortably fit it all into our days; we'd reached the balance we wanted and everything felt manageable.

Now we have children, life is no longer as simple as work hard, play hard. We have little people who are demanding on our time and our hearts; we want to be with them as much as possible. Now that our children are in the mix, we simply can't spend as much time and give as much focus to each area of our lives as we did before; we need to make compromises.

Despite this, many of us still try, and then we beat ourselves up when we fail to deliver to our own high expectations. So, what is causing some of us to behave in this way?

The drivers that motivate us

Taibi Kahler, an American psychologist, identified five common drivers that motivate us. These drivers are born in our unconsciousness and influence our thinking, feelings and behaviours. While they can be positive, they can also be destructive when we are subjected to too much pressure.

The drivers are be perfect, be strong, hurry up, please others and try hard. We all have an element of each of them, but for each individual, some drivers are much stronger than others.

People with a strong 'be perfect' drive aim for excellence in everything they do. They often have a reputation for being hardworking, reliable and delivering to an exceptionally high standard. The drawback of having a strong 'be perfect' driver is that it can come hand in hand with a fear of failure. For mothers, this can mean focusing on delivering to the same standard as they did before they had children when they had much more time.

'Be strong' individuals are driven by the need to cope and remain calm, whatever the circumstances. Other people tend to feel safe around them, knowing that someone is taking charge, which makes this driver a wonderful quality for any parent. However, people with a dominant 'be strong' driver can be reluctant to ask for help when they need it, and they can be so focused on being strong that they let their need to cope overshadow others' need for emotional reassurance.

Those with a 'hurry up' style like to do everything as quickly as they possibly can. This is great for a working mother as 'hurry up' people have the ability to get a lot done in a short space of time. In fact, they tend to be energised by having a lot on and a couple of deadlines thrown in, but they do need to be careful that their desire for speed and efficiency doesn't spill over into all areas of their lives. Sometimes it's about enjoying the moment – time with their family rather than ploughing through the tasks in hand.

People who have a strong 'please others' driver are focused on the needs of those around them – what mother isn't? They use intuition and body language to read people and often hold the family together. On the down side, 'please others' individuals are sometimes reluctant to challenge the views or actions of others for fear of upsetting them.

'Try hard' people are full of energy and passion when it comes to completing the task in hand. They will do everything they can, they are fully committed to whatever job they take on, but 'try hard' people can find it difficult to say no and often take on too much. This means they can end up not being able to finish tasks.

The drivers that come naturally to you probably stood you in good stead before children, helping you to achieve great things in your professional and personal lives. Now there are so many demands on you, there is a need, even if only subconsciously, to adapt your behaviours to align with the needs of being a working mother. This can come more easily to some of us than others.

If any one of the drivers dominates, it can start driving behaviours that can prove problematic. We need to understand what is important to us, our families, and to those at work, to help us to be 'good' while allowing us a release from the shackles of trying to be perfect in everything we do.

Understand what really matters

Often, we obsess about things that genuinely aren't important because we have been socialised to attach value to those things. Rarely do men obsess about having a perfectly managed home; they don't attach the same value to it as women. The rare man who does is just a clean man, whereas when a woman doesn't, it is seen as a failing.

Unfortunately, I spent years judging myself on what I thought was important to my children. What I've found is that while I may be wracked with guilt for not being the parent I think they want, they are actually quite happy.

In the days before football took over his weekends, my son and I used to spend time together on a Saturday morning when my daughter went off to her climbing lessons. We loved that time. It was the one time of the week where it was just the two of us in the house, and we could do exactly what we wanted to before the routine of the weekend beckoned.

One Saturday, I had what I deemed to be the best morning planned out. There was a robot exhibition on at the Science Museum. We would go into London together, spend a few hours wandering around before heading back – one-to-one time where I could really focus on him and be the mother I thought he wanted. It was what I wanted, and I thought it was what my son and I needed.

My son, on the other hand, was adamant he wanted to go for a bike ride. He wanted to cycle up to our local bakers, and then take the fresh pastries we bought to the park and tuck into them as we sat together on one of the benches. But surely this would mean I wasn't being the absolute best mother I could be?

I tried to negotiate, persuade him that going to the exhibition would be far better for the two of us, but his mind was set. I was conscious that his routine in the week was dominated by pulls from school, swimming lessons, homework – the simple reality of having two parents who work; I therefore always allowed him to heavily influence what we did when we had time together like this. So up we got. We went through the palaver of getting the bikes out of the shed, me biting my lip, not saying anything, smiling and being the mother (on the outside) I wanted to be. Off we went, cycling to the small lane of shops nearby.

Suddenly I noticed the blue sky and the sun shining; I could feel the warmth on my face in the spring sunshine. My son was animated, relaxed and chatting merrily to me, filling me in on his week. We picked up the pastries, headed to the park and sat on a bench, exactly as he had planned, eating contentedly in each other's company.

He had instinctively known what he wanted, what would make him happy, and actually what would make me happy. I just needed to listen to him to be the mother he needed me to be.

The easiest way to find out what our children think makes us a good mother is to ask them and listen to them. When they are young, we have to guess a little, but the older they become, the more clearly they can articulate their needs themselves.

If this isn't an easy conversation to have, which it isn't in many households, choose a time when your children are relaxed and the conversation won't feel confrontational. Children open up more when you aren't looking directly at them, so a conversation when you're in the car or when you are on a walk may work better for you. Then just listen to what they say; don't talk or interrupt. This is the single most important part of helping your children open up. When they've spoken, reflect back what they're saying so they know you have listened and understand.

Once you know what is important to your children, if you need to make compromises, ensure the whole family is involved in making them and everyone feels part of it. Talk about what you are able to do, as well as what you are always going to find more difficult because you work. Explain that although you may not be able to take them to ballet or rugby on a Thursday evening, for example, you can go for a family walk at the weekend with the promise of a drink and crisps at the end of it. I have agreed with my children that I won't go on any more school trips with them where we don't actually spend much time together, but I will always take an inset day off so I can spend the whole day with them.

At work, use the phrase 'work smarter, not harder' as your mantra. Ask your leaders, stakeholders and peers what will make you successful in your role. Again, really listen to what they say rather than assuming.

In the paper '15 Traits of The Ideal Employee',[9] Forbes explains ideal employees share some common traits. These traits include, but are not limited to, people who can be described as action-orientated, intelligent, ambitious, autonomous, leaders, fit culturally, upbeat, confident, successful, honest, detail orientated, modest, hardworking, marketable and passionate. What's interesting is that none of these are time dependent. These are all about having integrity, strong values and principles that we hold close, irrespective of what we are doing.

As working mothers, we need to know what's important at work and then figure out how to use our strengths to reach our goals in the quickest and most efficient way possible.

MAKING IT WORK

Maria, mother to Isha and Ali, gift shop owner

Maria has a naturally dominant 'be perfect' driver and has to work hard to suppress it so that it doesn't become problematic. She watches herself every day to make sure it doesn't get out of control and regularly

---

9   '15 Traits Of The Ideal Employee', Ken Sundheim, Forbes 2013

challenges herself on whether she is over-delivering. When this driver has an impact on how much time she spends with her children, she feels unhappy, but she keeps reminding herself of what's important in each area of her life and tries to relax a bit on everything else.

For example, she makes sure she's home to eat dinner with the children as often as she can, and she tries not to let it bother her when her house isn't tidy and she's not opened the post for the last four days. Above all, she tries her hardest to have faith in herself and her abilities.

Maria has found that accepting that good is good enough hasn't resulted in her failing at everything; in fact, it's the opposite. She's really enjoying developing her business and she's confident she's a good mother to her children because they tell her she is, and theirs is the only opinion that matters.

Some ideas to try

- Identify which drivers motivate you. There are a number of online questionnaires which will help you identify your dominant drivers (search Taibi Kahler drivers questionnaire).

- Talk to your children and your work colleagues to understand what they really need from you. This will help you to know how to genuinely satisfy them and relax a little on everything else.

- Try completing something to a lesser standard than usual – see if there are any real consequences other than your own perception of doing a good job.

- Don't let the fear of not being able to do something brilliantly stop you giving it a go. Remember that others will probably not have as high an expectation of you as you do of yourself, so view yourself through their eyes.

- Stop comparing yourself against people around you. Set your own standards for what works for you, your children and your job.

4
Principle Two – Live In The Moment

'Life exists only at this very moment, and in this moment it is infinite and eternal.'
— Alan Watts

When you are a working mother, with all of the responsibilities that brings, it can be easy to rush through life without seeing the beauty of what's right in front of you.

The philosophy of living in the present, or mindfulness as it's often called, has become hugely popular over the last decade. Mindfulness is the ability to rest in the here and now, engaged in whatever you are doing. It's praised for lowering stress levels, reducing blood pressure, even relieving pain such as migraines, but the benefits are wider reaching than just our physical wellbeing.

When we are living in the present:

- We are calm – the swirl of our thoughts and worries is reduced. We don't react to every thought, emotion and impulse, thereby reducing our anxiety, negativity and conflicting states of mind.

- We understand that thoughts are simply thoughts, not reality. We are able to become observers of these thoughts and accept them without judgment or pushing them away.

- Our performance and effectiveness increase. We are more alert, aware, creative and resourceful.

- Our relationships are stronger. When we are physically present, we are also mentally present and not distracted by our thoughts. Drifting occasionally is inevitable, but we can note this and gently return to the present. We are more aware of our needs and the needs of others; we listen more and give those around us our full attention. People sense that we are fully with them.

What prevents us from being mindful?

How good are you at living in the present? Have you ever experienced moments where you are in the car and can't remember getting from A to B? You were on auto-pilot? Times when you were talking to a friend on the phone while putting on a wash and making the dinner? Moments when you were spending time with your children while mentally updating your to-do list and thinking about everything else you should be doing?

We know we should be present, but it's often easier said than done. There are always things to do and worries which constantly pull against us as we try to enjoy the present moment.

We are programmed to live in the past and the future. As humans, we all naturally look to the past to reflect on our mistakes and understand how to avoid repeating them; this contributes to our learning in life. Regular reflection on how we have performed or acted is healthy. Conversely, our fears about the future help us to tackle and address actions in a way that will be beneficial for us, even when they are uncomfortable or unpleasant. This fear is an essential part of our lives; without it we wouldn't be motivated to save money for the future, maintain our health or invest in our education. But when thoughts of the past and future preoccupy and dominate, we miss out on our enjoyment of the present.

We also have a strong tendency to always be striving to attain the next goal. Marshall Goldsmith refers to our tendency to do this as the Western Disease.[10] He asks us to complete the sentence: 'I'll be happy when ____'. We might say, 'When I have paid off my mortgage',

10   Marshall Goldsmith, *Triggers*, 2016

'When I've gained the promotion' or even 'When I have put the children through university'. Goldsmith explains having an answer is actually just an illusion. As soon as we achieve one goal, the responsibility of another demands our attention.

Goals in themselves are healthy to have; they motivate us and keep us focused on the journey we want to take through life. But when we believe that achieving our goals will make us happy and fulfilled, we spend our lives trying to achieve them. This drives a tendency to fixate on the future at the expense of enjoying the life we're living now.

Life doesn't actually have a purpose at the end; it's all about the journey. Alan Watts, the twentieth-century philosopher, imagined life as a piece of music.

> 'When we listen to music it isn't about getting to the end of the piece, otherwise the best musicians would be the ones that played the fastest. Dancing isn't about getting to a certain point in the room, it's about the dance itself.'[11]

Beware the barrenness of a busy life

Busyness has turned into something we tend to hide behind.

---

11   www.youtube.com/watch?v=tJNKs9hmmlE

'How's it going?'

'Oh, you know, crazy busy.'

'Yeah, me too. I'm so busy in my job right now and then running the kids around, I don't remember what it's like to just relax.'

'Me neither. One day it'll calm down, eh?'

'Uh-huh, one day.'

A paper in the *Journal of Consumer Research*[12] argues that a busy and overworked lifestyle, rather than a leisurely lifestyle, has become an 'aspirational status symbol'. Studies show this is driven by 'perceptions that a busy person possesses desired human capital characteristics (eg competence and ambition)'. The paper talks about how these characteristics are in demand professionally, but many of us have translated them into desirable characteristics personally as well. I'm busy, therefore I'm important and valuable, therefore I'm worthy.

I was working from home one day. It was an opportunity to collect my son from school, which I do as often as I can, these opportunities are precious to me. At the last minute a conference call dropped

---

12 'Conspicuous Consumption of Time: When Busyness and Lack of Leisure Time Become a Status Symbol', Silvia Bellezza, Neeru Paharia, Anat Keinan.

into my diary. It was due to finish at 4.30 – exactly the time when I needed to collect my son from afterschool club. I joined the meeting, and while it was still going on, walked to school. Of course, the meeting overran, so when I arrived at the school gate at half past, the meeting was still going.

As soon as my son saw me, he started begging me for a playdate at his best friend's house. I had both him and his friend pleading with me as well as the meeting going on in my ears. I nodded I was happy for the playdate to go ahead. So, ironically, I then started walking away from the school, back home, without my son.

My friend Amanda grabbed me. She wanted to know if I could do a couple of slots on our class stall at the summer fête. I was desperately trying to hold on to the thread of the conversation going on in my ear as well as making sure I was not abrupt or rude to my friend, praying that no one would ask me a question on the call.

'Of course,' I said, 'I would love to.'

Walking through the park back home, I passed another friend, Sam. She talked to me about arrangements for that evening.

'Yes, I'll pick you up at seven o'clock, yes, yes, see you later on.' I waved goodbye.

There is rarely a wrong or right answer in these scenarios; you just have to trust yourself. I know I cram a huge amount into my days and weeks. I'm terrible at recognising when I've taken enough on and need to start saying no. When I take on too much, I tend to wake in the middle of the night with my mind racing, a swirl of thoughts going over what is coming up the next day. I struggle to concentrate fully and never feel that I'm doing anything well. Worst of all, my children know when I'm not really there. They challenge me when I'm on a device and they are trying to talk to me or I'm making the dinner while playing a game with them. They know when they don't have my full attention.

Our children always know when we are present and when we're not. In some ways, they are much more perceptive and less accepting than adults.

It's not that we shouldn't have full lives, but we do need to make sure we aren't taking too much on and using busyness as a way of hiding from the truth of our lives. Perhaps we feel guilty we aren't there for our children and family all of the time. We may fear being ordinary, or deep down, we know we aren't investing enough effort in our relationship with our partner. If we take a minute to stop, do these thoughts surface and become ones that we are afraid to properly address?

As Socrates said, 'Beware the barrenness of a busy life'. Make sure that you aren't hiding from an uncomfortable reality.

MAKING IT WORK

Ines, mother to Ava and Lucas, reflexologist

Ines divorced from her husband when her children were four and two. At the time, she wasn't working, but prior to becoming a mother, she was in PR. On a practical level, she needed to return to work after the divorce; she simply couldn't afford not to. At the same time, she was acutely aware the children were struggling to adjust to the divorce and new living arrangements whereby they lived with her half the week and every other weekend. She wanted to make sure that as far as she could, she wasn't working when the children were with her.

She has retrained as a reflexologist. This allows her to work for herself and, to a large extent, dictate her own hours. When the children are with her, she arranges to meet clients during school hours. When they are with her ex-husband, she throws herself into her work, crams in client sessions day and night, and catches up with paperwork and meets friends on her spare weekends. It's full on, and doesn't always work perfectly – she is running her own business, after all, but it gives her the time with her children that they all need.

Some ideas to try

- Slow down. We live at a pace we just aren't designed to experience, hurtling along with social media, emails, racing around to afterschool clubs and social events. Try slowing everything down.

- Practise mindfulness. It takes time to become skilled at mindfulness, so use an app to establish good meditation habits (I like Headspace).

- If mindfulness isn't for you, try going for a walk through green spaces or doing something creative instead. Either can hold your attention while at the same time allowing scope for reflection. In psychology, this is called involuntary attention. Simply going for a walk can calm the mind, offer new perspective and facilitate greater awareness. *Solvitur ambulando* is Latin for 'it is solved by walking'. As you walk, be aware of what you see, hear, smell, physical feelings, thoughts and emotions.

- Breathe well. We tend to take shallow breaths rather than long, deep breaths. Taking a deep breath calms us down by triggering neurons in our brains which tell our body it is time to relax. Breaths should be slow and rhythmic through the nose, circulating oxygen down to fill the lungs.

- Try breathing into your abdomen, not just your chest. Breathe in slowly for three to four seconds; your chest will slightly widen, your diaphragm will pull your chest cavity down and your belly button pulls away from your spine. When your lungs are full, exhale slowly and pull your belly button back in towards your spine to push out all of the air from the lungs for three to four seconds.

- Accept both positive and negative emotions. Mindful people don't push back on negative emotions, nor do they always look on the bright side. Feeling all emotions without resisting or controlling them will help you to maintain a balanced view of life and enable you to cope better with life's challenges.

5

Principle Three – Be Your Own Best Friend

'I was always looking outside myself for strength and confidence but it comes from within. It is there all the time.'
— Anna Freud

On days when the sun is shining, the children are behaving like angels and work is under control, we easily reflect on how we're doing a pretty good job overall. We smile and acknowledge everything we've achieved. Calm and gentle words towards ourselves come effortlessly on days such as these.

On the darker, tougher days, it's a totally different story. Life feels like one long slog; nothing goes the way we want or expect it to. Our attitude towards ourselves is now completely different. We judge ourselves, remember all of our faults and berate ourselves for them, blaming ourselves for what's going on around us. The internal voices are harsh and lack kindness and sympathy.

We use unkind words towards ourselves which we would never use towards a friend seeking comfort. We would never criticise their capability or pass judgment, saying they should have known better. We would reassure them, remind them that we all make mistakes. To fail and plain mess up is normal. We would help them put the situation into context and remind them what amazing people they are.

Self-compassion

We all know how to be a good friend, we all possess the necessary skills of friendship, but when we need support and comfort ourselves, we can be harsh and judging when we need love and support the most.

Many of us are familiar with self-confidence and self-esteem. Self-confidence is a belief that we can succeed at something, such as playing the piano or presenting to large groups of people. We can increase our self-confidence through practice and mastering a particular activity.

Self-esteem is the value we see ourselves having in the world. It's pretty consistent over our whole lives as it's based on a broad sense of personal value or self-worth. We are all encouraged to value high self-esteem, yet we also know logically we can't all be above average in everything we do. It is now thought that aspiring to high self-esteem can encourage narcissism and distorted self-perception because society doesn't accept us being average and much of our self-esteem is built on what we can accomplish.

Self-compassion, on the other hand, is about viewing ourselves subjectively and simply relating to ourselves with kindness in the same way we would a valued friend. It is a concept derived from Buddhist psychology and literally means 'to suffer with'. It gives us emotional resilience, a more realistic view of ourselves, and develops our ability to have more caring relationships. Self-compassion isn't about self-pity, wrapping ourselves in our own individual drama, and it doesn't have the same drawbacks as self-esteem. At its most basic level, it helps us to be our own best friend.

When we show ourselves self-compassion, we:

- Reflect on the context of our troubles. We remember that everyone else in the world experiences the ups and downs of life; it is all perfectly normal and part of living a good and full life.

- Don't judge ourselves.

- Accept we all make mistakes. As humans, it's inevitable. The important thing is to pick ourselves up, learn from them, forgive ourselves and move on.

- Are aware of our own feelings during the difficult times. We acknowledge that the moment is painful and don't try to suppress or push away thoughts.

- Use language towards ourselves that is kind, sympathetic and supportive.

- Allow ourselves the time and space we need to recuperate.

Not so long ago, my son banged his foot at school one afternoon. The next morning, his toe was swollen; he needed to be seen by the doctor.

My husband was already at work. I had a big day ahead and it was going to be difficult for me to miss a morning's work. I was wracked with guilt, trying to work out whether it would make any difference if my husband took him to the doctor in the afternoon instead of me that morning. Then I decided the question I had to answer was whether my son or my job was more important. I had to stay with him.

My daughter immediately challenged me. 'Stop, Mummy. Let Daddy take him later. Send him to school for the morning, he'll be OK.'

I told her I felt like a terrible mother.

'You're not,' she said, 'you're a wonderful mother. This decision doesn't make you a bad mother.'

She's always been wise beyond her years.

I rethought the situation and let my daughter's reassurance persuade me to take him into school. I then began walking to the Tube station, still judging myself and the decision I had made. There were negative words and feelings circling around my head. I hated myself for leaving my son, knowing that many others would have made a different decision.

It was then that I bumped into my friend Madeleine, also on her way to work. I shared the story of my morning. She sympathised with my situation.

'It's not as easy as saying your child or your work is more important,' she said. 'Of course, your child is, but it's not as simple… ' The sentence went unfinished as she made a balancing gesture with her hands.

She understood, didn't judge me and offered me support and compassion. I felt so comforted by the conversation we had; it helped me to put everything into perspective and carry on with my day. My husband ended up taking my son for an X-ray that afternoon. He had a badly bruised toe, but nothing serious.

Reflecting back later that day, I could see more clearly that my decision was about me balancing my son's needs against my responsibilities at work. That didn't make me a bad mother. My son knows I love him and he is more important to me than work, but he also recognises that I need to take a sensible and balanced approach to family and work.

It was at that point that I was able to use kinder words towards myself – show self-compassion. My daughter and my friend had treated me kindly and supported my emotional needs, and I knew I needed to learn from this and be a better friend to myself.

Use guilt as a reminder

Mother guilt is where we have adverse feelings about working and a sense that we are short-changing our children and families for the sake of our careers – as well as short-changing our employers or careers by spending time with our children. It stems from a sense of obligation: that there is something we should be doing, but aren't. It can be toxic, making us feel terrible about the choices we make. We've all felt it at one time or another; it's palpable.

I'm not sure a day goes by without me feeling guilty at one point or another. The moment when I realise my children aren't being invited on playdates, I'm guessing it's because I struggle to be home in time to host them myself. Not making it to every school assembly or afterschool book reading because they're held at 3.15. The 'urgent' early morning meetings I don't make because I can't find childcare. I hold myself responsible for the fact that my son doesn't do as well as he could in his spelling tests because I haven't been at home enough to dedicate the time with him to practise. When I'm out with work in the evening, I feel guilty for not being at home. When I miss a work event to stay at home, I feel guilty for not being committed enough to my work. Guilty when I send my children to school feeling unwell, or when I respond to work messages when I'm with my children.

Does any of this sound familiar?

At its best, guilt is the emotional equivalent of physical pain: a warning sign that something's overloaded, some unseen damage is being done. Guilt gives us a good old nudge when we are not paying an area or relationship in our lives enough attention. It reminds us what is important, helps us keep track of what's owed when, and to whom.

The contented working mother can distinguish between toxic guilt and a healthy reminder and make sure the toxic guilt doesn't influence her thinking and decision making. She pushes it aside and remembers the Harvard study which found that the daughters of working mothers go on to have more successful careers and more equal relationships, and that sons of working mothers end up having a greater role in the home.

As much as I know I shouldn't, I've sometimes let toxic guilt influence me and my decisions over the years. I know exactly how hard it is to manage. I feel guilty about writing this book when I could be spending time with my children. I feel guilty when I push my poorly children into school when many mothers would decide to keep theirs at home. Sometimes I go so far as dosing them with paracetamol to bring their temperatures down before sending them in, waving them off with a cheery, 'Get school to call me if you're actually sick' so I can make that 'super-important' meeting on the other side of town.

Not so long ago, I went away on a girls' weekend and didn't see my children from the Thursday evening to Monday morning. On the Monday morning, my son awoke telling me how terrible he felt. I know that if I hadn't been away for the weekend, I would have packed him off to school, but the guilt I felt about taking time out for myself (which was amazing and well worth it) meant that my usual approach was weakened. He knew this and made the most of it. I felt like I was between a rock and a hard place. I wanted to look after my son properly but felt guilty for being out of the office for so long already.

I decided to deal with it from a purely logistical perspective. I left him with my cleaner who was coming that morning, which allowed me to dash into work, attend a couple of meetings, show my face and dash home again. I ended up running around like a mad thing, leaving my son feeling emotionally abandoned and short-changing everyone and everything.

Working mothers regularly experience situations where they can find no wrong or right answer. It's a dilemma; often there *is* no right answer.

MAKING IT WORK

Jen, mother to Grace and James, PA

Jen's job involves long hours and can be stressful at times. When she became a mother, she found she was, like many working mothers, trying to fit more and more into her day. All too often, Jen found that when it was feeling too much, she put aside her 'me time' activities, like taking the dog for a walk on her own, or her exercise routine.

She realised that although it was easy to justify this decision in her head, giving her more time to finish work commitments or allowing her more time with the children, it meant she no longer had the activities in her life that truly cleared her head and re-energised her. Jen now fiercely protects the things that help her relax. She knows that ultimately they help her to be the mother she wants to be with her children and be her best at work.

Some ideas to try

- At the end of a tough day, reflect on the voices in your head. Are you being harder on yourself than you would be with a good friend? Change any negative, destructive language into positive. Have sympathy, comfort yourself and remind yourself that tomorrow is another day.

- Never blame the fact that you are a working mother for hard times at home. They happen irrespective of whether you work or not. How many of you have beaten yourselves up when your children are misbehaving, thinking that if you weren't working, it wouldn't have happened? Yes, it would. When I listen to my girlfriends' experiences, I realise we're all going through the same things, irrespective of whether we work or not. We must have confidence that the decisions we have made are the right ones and not let the twists and turns make us question our choices.

- Write down kind things friends and colleagues say about you. When you're going through a rough patch, reread the messages and let them have the same powerful and positive effect they did originally.

- Forgive yourself when you mess up; don't be overly hard on yourself. As Alexander Pope said, 'To err is human; to forgive, divine.'

- Every day, compliment yourself on three things you have done well.

6

Principle Four – Be Resilient Every Day

'If every choice you make comes from an honest place, you're solid, and nothing anybody can say about you can rock you or change your opinion.'
— Angelina Jolie

Resilience equips us to deal with life's inevitable ups and downs. When we have high resilience, we can cope with the bruises we get from living life. We are able to pick ourselves back up, smile and carry on, knowing it's all just part of the richness of life.

When we aren't fully equipped to deal with the pressures of life, stress builds up. If we don't manage the stress, eventually, we reach a point where it takes a toll on us physically and mentally. Our sleep can become disrupted, switching off becomes more difficult; we may turn to drinking or smoking to help us relax. It may even manifest itself in physical symptoms of tension, maybe a knot in our stomachs, a headache or tension in our neck or shoulders. Ultimately, it can affect our behaviour, and the last thing any of us want to do is to snap at those we love.

The different types of stress we face

The day to day. We often talk about how we need resilience against a 'thing', an 'incident', but as working mothers, we face challenges every single day. When we take too much on, this can cause us stress.

Possible stress points – a meeting overrunning and making you late to pick up your children; the children playing up when you have to get into work for an important meeting; having to create a snail costume for little Freddie's assembly with two days' notice.

The unexpected. Sometimes something unanticipated and out of the ordinary happens, but everyone still expects the same level of commitment from us. The family still needs feeding, bills still need to be paid, but we haven't been able to plan for this additional dynamic.

Possible stress points – illness of someone in the family; last-minute work trip; being made redundant.

A slow build up. Sometimes the stress builds up so slowly and over such a long time period, we don't notice it's happening at first. Many minor causes of stress, which we can manage perfectly well for a short period, can overwhelm us when we are carrying them for a prolonged period of time or alongside other stresses.

Possible stress points – increase in workload; deteriorating relationship with your boss or partner; general unhappiness in your job.

I was caught out a few months ago by all three types of stress coinciding. Work was pretty full on at the time, but manageable. Then my son's eardrum burst. Not a big drama, or so we thought until it became infected. He became seriously ill and ended up in hospital for four days. During that week, I continued to work while my husband did the day shift. I then returned to hospital every afternoon to be with my son for the end of the day and sleep overnight with him.

Holding down my nine-to-five job while looking after my son became extremely difficult, but I didn't recognise how stressful I was finding it. I graciously declined offers of help from my parents (madness) and kept going. I drew on my resilience like crazy to make it through that week, and on the surface, I coped just fine, thank you very much. In fact, more than fine; my husband and I kept going with all the usual things in life as well. My daughter had a sleepover for her birthday (she had been so amazing that week, I hadn't wanted to cancel), we finalised holiday bookings, fed ourselves – life carried on.

My son recovered, life started to get back to normal, but soon afterwards, work became all consuming. I genuinely love my work, which actually is part of the problem as it makes it much more difficult for me to notice when things become too much. The consultancy where I work was preparing for an event with about 150 people. As part of the event, I was giving a talk, and I found this effort on top of my full-time client work hard. My stress levels reached a point where my back froze up, I wasn't sleeping properly and my head was constantly spinning with everything I had to do. I had taken on so much but was feeling like I wasn't achieving anything.

It took a friend over a coffee a few weeks later to point out to me that I had never given myself a break after my son's illness. I realised that I'd forgotten how important it is to look after myself and keep my resilience strong. I know I'm a pretty resilient person, but that knowledge meant I'd become complacent and completely lacked any awareness of how stressed I'd become during this difficult period. I decided to create the time and space to look after myself a bit better, allowing myself to heal and recover.

I look back and know the reason I had missed the signs was that, apart from my son being in hospital,

I wasn't actually unhappy. It was the volume of work that pushed me over the edge.

Work out how resilient you are. There are a number of questionnaires online which assess whether you have a healthy view of yourself, use humour during hard times, have friends you can talk to and are good at solving problems. It is worth finding one that is based on Al Siebert's resilience questionnaire.[13] Siebert spent much of his career developing the thinking behind psychological resilience and is considered an expert in the field.

Even if you score highly, you have to work hard to maintain your resilience. I generally score highly, but my earlier story shows we can never become complacent.

If you are feeling stressed

Seek help. If you feel that you aren't managing and you are stressed, talk to a friend or go and see your doctor. Don't ignore the signs.

Compartmentalise the stress. The activities or 'things' causing you stress don't need to affect every area of your life. If your boss is making your life a misery, you can still enjoy (and need more than ever) a good night out with friends. On the other side, if you are going

---

13 'How Resilient Are You?' www.resiliencyquiz.com

through a rough patch at home, be thankful you have your work to distract you. Don't feel guilty that you are taking enjoyment from other areas of your life, or that you are using them as an escape until you get fully back on track.

Know when to walk away. There's a story (I'm not sure of the origin) about a university professor of psychology who was in a lecture one day. She picked up a glass of water and asked everyone, 'How heavy is this glass of water?'

The students called out various answers, which the professor shrugged off. 'The actual weight doesn't matter,' she explained to them. 'What really matters is how long I've been holding it. If I hold it for just a minute, it feels light. If I hold it for an hour, I'll have an ache in my arm. If I hold it for a whole day, my arm will feel numb and paralysed. Any longer than that and I will be tempted to give up and drop it. In each case, the weight of the glass doesn't change, but the longer I hold it, the heavier it becomes.'

The professor continued, 'The stresses and worries in life are like this glass of water. Carry them for only a short while and they're manageable. Worry about them a bit longer and they begin to hurt. And if we think about them all day long, or longer, we can feel paralysed and hopeless – incapable of concentrating or focusing on anything else.'

For a while, we don't really notice that the stress is weighing us down. But when we carry it around for days, weeks, months, it can become more than we can bear. The glass represents the stresses in our lives. It's important to know when we need to put the glass down.

I once had a job I truly loved and that suited me down to the ground. But times changed. I started working for a man who didn't understand what I did and turned my job into something he did understand, but one that I didn't want. I felt like a square peg in a round hole.

It became more and more difficult to keep going; I became extremely stressed. I reached the point where it was affecting me physically and mentally. Walking towards the entrance of the office made my eyes well up with tears (and I'm not normally an emotional person at work). My skin was in a state, my hair was falling out, and no matter how much I tried to leave my stress at the front door when I arrived home, I couldn't. It changed my behaviour at home; my children could see the effect it was having on me. The last thing I wanted was for my job to have an impact on them. Nor did I want them to think it was acceptable for me to tolerate the situation; that wasn't the role model I wanted to be to them.

It took me a while to work it out, but eventually I realised that I had to put the stress down. I had to look after my own physical and mental health and my relationships with my family. I left the organisation and walked away from the stress. It was hard, but absolutely the right decision to make.

MAKING IT WORK

Caroline, mother to Ella, Poppy and Oliver, primary school teacher

Caroline trained as a solicitor. After she started practising, she realised she had only embarked on the career because it was expected of her. She had never explored what her options were, and more importantly, what she really wanted to do.

When she had children, things became really tough. The hours, the workload and the stress that came with them meant that she wasn't able to dedicate the time she wanted to her young children. When she looked around, she could see other women enjoying the same career alongside family life, and she struggled to understand why she wasn't coping. The stress became unbearable and she eventually had a nervous breakdown.

The reason she was finding it so stressful was because, deep down, she didn't want to be a solicitor; it didn't align with her values. She left her job and trained as a teacher. She is now happy and fulfilled in her professional life as well as at home – her job aligns fully with her values.

Some ideas to try

- Make sure the core parts of your life align with your values and what makes you happy. If you have a job that you don't love or doesn't sit comfortably with your values, things will feel much more difficult.

- Surround yourself with supportive friends and family. When you are going through a tough patch, talk to them; lean on them. After a really hard day at work, is there anything better than walking through the door and feeling little arms wrapping themselves around you and being told how much you're loved? Or a night out with the girls? Allow yourself to be distracted and laugh with your friends and family.

- Prioritise your physical and mental health. Take exercise, eat healthily, practise mindfulness. Not only will this increase your quality of life today, but it is thought to decrease your chances of getting serious diseases later in life.

- Establish a good sleep routine. Insufficient sleep has severe effects on our physical and mental wellbeing, and therefore our resilience. Sleep is a privilege. Resilient people respect their sleep; they never take it for granted.

- Take all your annual leave entitlement (and buy more if you can). In 2016, 40% of the British workforce did not use their full holiday entitlement,[14] losing on average five days of annual leave each year. Time off work is our way of fully connecting with our families, of giving ourselves a true break, resulting in better wellbeing and potentially improving performance and creativity.

Many of us cite having 'too much work on' as a reason for not taking time off, but studies by consulting firms Boston Consulting Group and Ernst & Young show that more than 80% of employees who take their leave report a positive impact on morale and more than 70% report increases in productivity.

---

14 From www.consultancy.co.uk 'Overworked Britons wasted 163 million annual leave days in 2016'. Based on research commissioned by holiday firm Airtours and leveraged from the Employment and Labour Market survey performed by the UK's Office of National Statistics (ONS)

7
Principle Five – Believe In Yourself

'I've learned that whenever I decide something with an open heart, I usually make the right decision.'
— Maya Angelou

Believing in yourself and holding a strong positive mindset is essential to being a contented working mother. Positive emotions like love and joy help us to broaden our thinking and open our eyes to more opportunities. We are more creative, our self-confidence increases and our stress levels are reduced.

When we believe in ourselves, we naturally have a more positive and optimistic view of life. We radiate joy and hope. As a result, we become more attractive to be with. People tend to gravitate towards positive people and keep a distance from negative people. Positive people are more fun to be around.

Why we feel negative sometimes

The idea of basic emotions dates back as far as the *Book of Rites*, a first-century Chinese encyclopaedia that identifies seven 'human feelings': joy, anger, sadness, fear, love, disliking and liking. Although the thinking around this has developed over the years, it hasn't deviated far from the idea of these as our basic emotions. Interestingly, four out of the seven are negative.

Not only are more of our basic emotions negative, but this pattern follows through to our language as well. There are far more words in the English language to express negative emotions than positive and we are more inclined to engage more deeply with these emotions. When we are experiencing a positive emotion, we know everything is under control and no action is needed. On the other hand, negative emotions are warning us that there is something wrong, so we naturally give them more attention, time and energy to resolve the issues we are facing. When we read all this, it can be hard to believe that any of us manages to think positively with the odds stacked against us like this. But we do; we all have positive thoughts, albeit in differing proportions. We all want to believe in ourselves.

Steps to develop a stronger self-belief

There are five easy steps you can take to develop a stronger belief in yourself.

Step 1: Banish the imposter. Many working mothers feel like downright frauds, their accomplishments only having come about as the result of chance and luck. This psychological phenomenon is known as 'imposter syndrome'. It's a belief that we are inadequate and incompetent, despite evidence that indicates we're skilled and successful.

If you experience feelings of waiting to be 'found out', try these techniques to help you.

- Amy Cuddy advises us in her TED talk of the same name to 'Fake it till you make it'[15]. Behave and act as though you are the person you want to be, until you actually are.

- Remember that no one knows what they are doing all the time. There are lots of people who profess to know all the answers, but they really don't. The best and bravest of us are experimenting, failing, trying again and succeeding once in a while.

- Keep a record of positive things others say about you and reflect back on the record in times of need.

---

15 Amy Cuddy 'Fake it 'til you make it,' www.youtube.com/watch?v=R VmMeMcGc0Y&list=PLqlSNxscEHTxrBGjGnotv0sz9tfzuTT5B

I battle with imposter syndrome every single day I work. Irrespective of the fact that on one level, I'm proud of what I've achieved, I struggle to believe that I haven't reached this point in my career purely because of luck and help from people around me.

Step 2: Nurture your growth mindset. It takes talent and an incredible amount of hard work to become great at something. Jessica Ennis-Hill has an inherent talent for athletics, but she also practised relentlessly, determined to be the best. It's easy to look at the achievements of exceptional people and think their success comes from their innate gifts, but it doesn't really; there's always a lot of hard work behind their success.

We develop a self-belief of the person we are as a result of our past experiences, our successes and failures and the expectations of those around us. Sometimes we create limiting belief systems and then act in accordance with these, but we don't need to let the experiences of our past limit or define our future.

A fixed mindset is one that assumes abilities and understanding are relatively fixed across people's lives. With a fixed mindset, we believe we 'have it or we don't' when it comes to abilities and talents. A growth mindset is one where we believe that abilities and understanding can be developed with time and effort. People rarely sit in one or the other of these exclusively and often have a fixed mindset with respect to one area of their lives (they may be convinced they have no musical aptitude) and be open to growth in a different area of their lives.

When it comes to being a contented working mother, everyone can improve and become more skilled. To do so, focus on:

- Finding a job you are passionate about. It's easier to succeed when you are passionate about what you are doing.

- Becoming more aware of your talents, strengths and weaknesses.

- Viewing failure as an opportunity to learn from your experiences.

- Committing to becoming a lifelong learner. Be curious about the world in the same way a child is.

Step 3: Focus on what you can influence. Epictetus was a Greek Stoic Philosopher, born around 55AD. He theorised that all external events are beyond our control, so we should accept them calmly and dispassionately. Instead, we should focus on our own actions which we can control.

Almost 2,000 years later, this still makes absolute sense. We can't control the fact that our child's class assembly is being held at the same time as an important meeting that's been scheduled for a month, that the roads are icy and we can't drive to work, or our child's moody that day, yet we often feel responsible for everything working brilliantly in our home and work lives, irrespective of whether we can truly influence it or not.

We can't totally eliminate all of the challenges we face as working mothers, but we can influence them on a smaller scale through our own behaviours and actions. Remember the three challenges that working mothers face?

- Society isn't always on our side – we can't change the way the media portrays working mothers, but we can be a role model and shift perceptions of our peers, family and friends

- We live in a complex world – we can't make the world a simpler place to be, but we can experiment and keep learning to find out what works best at each point in time

- Inequality in the home – we can't affect what happens in other homes, but we can shift the balance in our own

Our energy and time are finite. If we spend them trying to influence the things beyond our control, we won't be successful and we will lose faith in who we are.

Let go of any worry associated with the challenges. Whatever you do, you can't eliminate them; there is no magic wand. Alan Watts likened life to a moving stream of water. As we are inevitably pushed downstream, we often fight against the flow – fighting something we cannot control. Instead, Watts urges us to notice the stream, the movement of it, and learn how to go with it rather than fighting.

Step 4: Stop comparing yourself against other people. It's not realistic to compare yourself to other people. Everyone has different commitments, different pulls on their time. Some people may be able to make assembly, sports day and go on school trips more easily than you. Your work colleagues won't all have to rush out of the door as regularly as you, nor will they necessarily get calls from school asking them to collect a seven-year-old who has just banged their head in the playground.

I went around to a friend's house a few months ago. She must have had 100 tomato plants in her kitchen which she had grown from seed for the school fête. I immediately felt inadequate and had to give myself a good shake to remind myself that there was no one else judging me on whether I was putting as much effort in for my own fête; it was me alone placing that pressure upon myself.

Step 5: Be proud of being a working mother. Being a contented working mother (or being on the journey to becoming one) is an amazing achievement. It's really tough and you're doing it. Be proud of that. I have spent too many years apologising for being a working mother, fearing others would judge the decisions I've made or my commitment to my job or my children.

I'm uncomfortable admitting this, but I used to omit to tell people that I was part time. Because I worked two half days as part of my four-day-week job, people around me didn't realise, but in reality, I wasn't doing the right thing for myself by keeping quiet, and I certainly wasn't doing the right thing for other women around me. Instead of constantly feeling I should be apologising for being part time, I should have been shouting from the rooftops that I'd reached a senior position in an organisation while being part time and a mother. I should have been sharing and celebrating the fact that I was proving the job could be done on a part-time basis and being a visible role model for other mothers.

I'm confident that irrespective of the fact that I work, my children are happy, and I know I'm committed and good at my job. I won't let anyone take that away from me, and I am proud of what I've achieved in life and that I'm making it as a contented working mother.

MAKING IT WORK

Sarah, mother to Sofia, accountant

Since becoming a mother, Sarah has totally redefined the expectations she sets for herself in the different areas of her life. She regularly reminds herself that she can't be everything to everyone and it's about being a contented working mother, not about excelling in any one area.

She openly admits she forgets sometimes and pushes in one area too much. She stays up late into the evening, working to make sure the report she's writing is the best it can possibly be. Or she spends hours decorating cupcakes for the cake sale at school.

Once she's realised what's happening, she gives herself a good shake and reminds herself that it's about the whole of her life, not one particular area. She puts down the report, assuring herself that it's good enough, and she asks her daughter to help her decorate the ready-made cupcakes she bought. She knows it's important to keep subtly adjusting her approach to how she lives her life.

Some ideas to try

- Take a piece of paper and a pen and write down any achievements you're proud of in your life. It may be completing a diploma while the kids were tiny, getting the promotion you'd been working so hard for, or that your kids are grounded and happy in their lives. Think of big and small achievements, then look back and reflect on how well you've done.

- Surround yourself with positive people. Happiness is catching.

- Take time alone to contemplate your life and recharge. One of my joys in life (albeit rare) is being able to go off for the day for a long walk in the countryside with my camera. I find a huge sense of freedom and calm from being on my own, having physical space around me and mental calm to process everything.

- Remember that there is no correlation between the guilt that working mothers feel and whether your children are happy.

- Adjust your attitude towards social media and recognise it for what it is – a great way to connect with friends and communities, but not something which should affect how you feel about yourself. Looking at pictures of mothers making incredible birthday cakes, making fancy Halloween costumes and partying all night on social media can give you a misleading view of others' lives. Make sure it doesn't result in you negatively reflecting on your own.

PART THREE
THE WORKING MOTHER'S SKILLS

8

Skill One – Make Everything Visible

'It is not enough to do your best; you must know what to do, and then do your best.'
— W. Edwards Deming

The more you keep in your head, the more ways you have for managing all of your activities, the more difficult it is to manage everything. When you don't have the right tools and efficient ways of approaching your activities, tasks and work, you can't tell when you've taken on too much, prioritise effectively, or distinguish your urgent tasks from the less important. Inevitably, you'll drop something at some point. No one wants to be in the position where they forget a deadline for a key customer report, or let their children down because they forgot that it is non-uniform day (you *never* want your child to be that kid at the school gates).

Sociological studies confirm that in the majority of family households, mothers draft the to-do lists while fathers pick and choose which tasks to do, so women take on most of the burden. Although many men are gradually taking on more in the house, women continue to be responsible for the detailed non-routine tasks, large and small, such as sending a note into school when a child has been ill, making doctors' appointments, scheduling afterschool clubs, buying uniforms, arranging snacks – the responsibilities are endless. We talk about overscheduling the children but forget we are also overscheduling ourselves.

Years ago, I used to carry notebooks around with me. I had one for work and one for home. They were filled with 'stuff' from my head: half-completed lists, reminders and phone numbers. To a certain extent, this system worked; it helped me keep all of my work or home thoughts, to-do lists and activities all in one place. But I was reliant on having them with me all the time, and what they didn't do was help me prioritise or manage how much work I was taking on at any point in time. With hindsight, I can see that I always took on too much and worked fairly inefficiently.

How much of your work can you see today? Do you have piles of folders, stickies on the fridge, notes left all over your desk, reminders in your email inbox? A book containing everyone's birthdays; a shopping list; to-do lists, one for work and one for home? Is there a mass of stuff in your head: the things that you haven't had the chance to do anything with yet?

It takes large reserves of emotional energy to stay on top of our family and professional duties. And the volume of this work isn't going to diminish. The tasks are never-ending and the mental load we need to stay on top of it all can feel overwhelming. We need to take a sensible and proven approach to manage it all effectively.

When we visualise all of our work, we envision the actions necessary to achieve a desired outcome. We are able to manage priorities and the amount of work in progress, meaning that we can be as efficient as possible. If we don't, we risk dropping things.

Many years ago, before I had fully honed the working mother principles and skills, I didn't turn up to a pantomime that a large group of us had booked. I had so many things in my head so I hadn't put it in my diary and had simply forgotten it. I now make sure I put any event straight into my diary, even though my friends make sure they remind me before what has become our annual pantomime 'just in case', and I haven't missed one since.

Visualising your responsibilities

The first skill will make all of your responsibilities and then your tasks across your professional and personal life visible.

We are going to think about our responsibilities. These are the things that we are accountable for in our homes and at work. They will include responsibilities like maintenance of the garden, delivery of the marketing strategy, budget planning. And then we will define our tasks. The smaller day-to-day pieces of work that ultimately support our responsibilities.

Time to make yourself a cup of tea. You will need some sticky notes or pieces of paper, a pen and a little peace and quiet.

I'm naturally a visual person so I like to do this exercise with some sticky notes, a good felt tip pen and a big space where I can lay everything out. Use whatever you have to hand – a kitchen table, a wall, perhaps the floor. If you have a whiteboard, that works really well too. Make sure there are no distractions; don't try to do this exercise while there are other people in the house or you're waiting for the plumber to arrive.

Although we need to view life as a whole, most of us usually have a relatively clear divide between work time and personal time, so it may help you to consider professional and personal responsibilities separately in this exercise. It helps me as I personally like to separate work and home as much as I can (recognising that there are a lot of blurred edges these days).

Start by writing down all of your home-based responsibilities. Use one sticky note for each responsibility. Include everything from keeping the house clean to one-off projects like redesigning a room.

To give you some ideas, my home responsibilities include:

The trick with this exercise is when you think you've exhausted everything, stay put. Spend another few minutes really teasing out everything from your head.

Now repeat the exercise for your work life. What you include here will really depend on your particular profession, but some examples are:

Take a photo of these two groups.

Now, take your sticky notes and separate them into one of the following four groups (keeping work and personal separate if that's how you completed the first part of the exercise).

Everything you want to do yourself – these are the responsibilities that align with your core values in life. They bring you a sense of satisfaction, instilling calm and contentment in you when you spend time on them.

When we spend time on the things we love, we are mentally happier, more likely to succeed at work, and we will be calmer mothers.

Everything you can stop – we're often so busy 'doing', it's hard to view our responsibilities objectively and challenge ourselves on whether they are still needed. They are part of our lives and it's easy to assume that we still need them in the same way we did a couple of years ago.

Everything you can share – we can't manage everything ourselves when we work; we need help. Behind every successful person there is always a support network. Florence Griffith Joyner had a team of coaches, trainers and dieticians; Barack Obama has Michelle; Michelangelo had a team of assistants helping him paint the Sistine Chapel. You also need a support network to be successful.

Everything else – these are the activities that you don't find any particular joy in, but you can't share them and are unable to stop them right now. There will be a number of responsibilities in this group, no doubt, but the aim is to minimise them by allocating them to different groups where you can.

There may well be a few raised eyebrows at this point. What responsibilities can you 'share'? Do you feel you can't afford professional help? That your partner or children won't help around the house beyond taking out the rubbish and making their beds? Sharing the workload and delegating may feel unrealistic, but it's critical if you are to have contentment in your life.

We will come back to these groupings in Skill #2.

Visualising your tasks

You're now going to visualise all of your current tasks: the smaller items that you need to do to ensure the smooth running of your home and work life. Take your sticky notes or pieces of paper and a pen. Find your space, and again, choose a time when you have no distractions.

Firstly, do this for your home tasks. Gather all the notes you've stuck on the fridge, scribbled in pads or on pieces of scrap paper; together with any lists that you use. Take a look at your email inbox and pull out actions behind emails. Write down everything you have in your head – I want you to get *everything* out there. Ignore any concerns about the sheer volume of work you are surfacing. I promise, this is going to help.

Your list will include items you need to remember to buy, things you need to remember to tell someone, appointments you need to arrange – everything. The sorts of activities to include are:

Take a look at it all – no doubt it's pretty overwhelming. That's OK, it will be. You are running a home, looking after children and working; you've got a lot on, so accept that you are always going to have a long list. There's no getting away from it. The key to success is facing into the reality and how we manage it.

Now repeat the exercise for your work tasks. As before, take time to make sure you include everything hidden in emails, on sticky notes on your desk, or in your head. The list should include everything from large projects to admin.

The sorts of things to include are:

Induction of new staff member

Get up to date with filing

Finalise brand options for new client

Book hotel for trip to Newcastle

Collate results of the engagement survey

Send analysis to Finance Team

Order stock for Easter

Reschedule appointments for Monday

Again, group these tasks. Keep a record of this exercise by taking another photo.

We will be looking at how to manage all your tasks on a day-to-day basis in Skill #3.

MAKING IT WORK

Rachael, mother to Amy, Megan and Joseph

Rachael has always found it difficult to switch off and often her head is still racing with thoughts of work while she is spending precious moments with her children in the evening. She knows it's impossible to draw a firm line between work and home in the days of 'always on' and that work will occasionally need her attention in the evenings and weekends, but she needs to build some guidelines to give herself the best possible chance of enjoying the time she has with her family.

Rachael has created no-work zones for herself where she doesn't check her phone or think about work – these are before she drops the children off at school in the morning, and between arriving home and the children's bedtime. She has also created a mantra for herself for when she arrives home. As she shuts her car door, she says 'Car door' to herself, then 'Garden door' as she shuts the garden gate and 'Front door' as she enters her home. With each phrase, she focuses on pushing work further and further behind her, knowing that she can tackle it again the next day.

Some ideas to try

- As soon as a task surfaces, capture it. Don't try to keep it in your head. Remembering everything in your head takes up precious and limited headspace.

- Mentally practise completing your most taxing tasks. Studies show that you can develop and improve real skills by visualising yourself practising them. Think of professional athletes training – they use visualisation because it really works.

- Check every few days to make sure that the scribbled lists and random notes aren't creeping back into your life.

9
Skill Two – Do Less

'Learn to let others do their share of the work.
Things may be done less well, but you will have
more peace of soul and health of body.'
   — Rose Philippine Duchesne

As teenagers, most of us only had to worry about ourselves. Anyone reading this who has a teenager will probably be reminded of this every day. Then, as we become independent adults, we move into our own homes. All of a sudden, we have new responsibilities: we have to pay bills, arrange maintenance of the house, maybe take on a mortgage. We meet someone, have children, develop our careers and try to find a little time for ourselves. Who would have guessed when we were naïve teenagers that life would feel so hard as adults?

Over the years, we take on more and more, yet we rarely take time to reflect and consider when we are doing too much. We need to recognise when it's time to take on less responsibility rather than more.

This is where the second working mother skill comes in. This skill is tough because for many of us, it goes against our natural inclination. We should be able to do everything, surely?

As well as working, running a home, supporting our children as they mature, many of us think we must have a home and garden worthy of an article in a glossy magazine and throw professional standard children's parties. It's just not possible, though; we aren't and shouldn't try to be superwomen. We need to learn to share responsibility and put stuff down. It's as simple, and as hard, as that.

It's time to take action

Time to make another cup of tea and find a quiet few minutes for yourself.

Look back at the responsibilities you visualised in the last chapter and work out whether you have taken too much on.

In the first skill, 'Make Everything Visible', you separated your responsibilities into four groups.

- Everything you want to do yourself
- Everything you can stop
- Everything you can share
- Everything else

That was the easy part. Now I want you to take a hard look at where you placed each sticky note. Do you have any in your 'everything I can stop' or 'everything I can share' groups? Really challenge yourself on whether you should be doing all your responsibilities to the extent you are today. If you can't stop them completely, can you reduce the amount of time you spend on them or bring in support to take some of the pressure off you?

Even if you've done this exercise before, you will still, when you really challenge yourself, be able to move responsibilities into the 'stop' and 'share more' groups. If you can't, ask a friend or your partner to help you with the exercise. Unless you move some of your responsibilities into these two groups, you won't be able to create more space in your life.

Everything you want to do yourself. These are the responsibilities that make you happy, so prioritise them. All too often, when we are under pressure, it's these responsibilities that we give up. Protect them fiercely and don't compromise your time on them. If you find peace while you're ironing, then hold on to it.

One for me at home is looking after the garden. I don't manage to find much time to focus on it, but when I do, I really enjoy tending to the plants and making it into an enjoyable place for the family to spend time. At work, it's coaching people. I find it rewarding and it's one of the responsibilities I make sure I create time for.

Everything you can stop. Congratulations for recognising that you need to stop some of the responsibilities in your life. Letting go may be a difficult process; you will need to decide whether you are able to stop immediately or whether you need to put some steps in place and step back gradually.

When my daughter was in Year 1, I became the Secretary for the school Parent Teacher Association (PTA). I loved helping to raise much-needed funds for the school; I helped out at fundraising events baking cakes, the school quiz and the school disco. As someone who didn't make it into school that much, I found it was a great way of connecting with the other parents as well.

While I was part time, it worked well. Once I moved to a full-time role, I had to accept I couldn't continue to commit my time in the same way and I stepped down in an official capacity. I still help out, but now on a much-reduced basis.

Everything you can share. Sit down with your partner and talk through where you are going to secure help from – either professionally or from them or other members of your family. By working through it with your partner, you are much more likely to engage them. Focus on making sure that the balance of responsibility in the home is fair. This will be different based on personal circumstances: whether one person travels a lot with work, how many days a week each of you work and so on.

If you are living in a world where the responsibilities of the home don't feel balanced at the moment, now is your opportunity to change that. When the only thing your partner does is ferry the boys to football on a Saturday morning, I appreciate that it will feel like a daunting and enormous shift, but it can be done, gradually and firmly.

Once you have worked out where you are going to secure more help from, you will need to think about how you are going to delegate. Delegating is a skill in itself, so you will find a section in Chapter 13 on how to delegate effectively.

Everything else. The reality is that there will be a number of responsibilities in this group. The aim is to continually challenge whether you can stop or share them to reduce the pressure on yourself. It's important to revisit and reflect on your responsibilities regularly to make sure that too much doesn't creep into this category again.

The support you need

There may be a number of reasons why you are struggling to secure the help you need.

You feel you can't afford professional help. It's easy to consider whether you can afford professional support based on your salary alone, but you need to think about it as a joint cost between you and your partner. Most of us instinctively calculate the cost against our salary because if we weren't working, it would be an expense we wouldn't need. This is factually true, but it would be the same if your partner wasn't working.

Ideally, we aren't working purely for money; we are investing in our professional futures, so if we are committed to our careers and our families, we have to think about investing in the running of the home where we can.

The second thing to think about when you're considering whether to take on professional help is just because you can do something yourself, it doesn't mean you should. When I returned to full-time work (after being part time), I didn't take on any extra help. Monday to Friday, I felt like I was getting further and further behind at home until I was overwhelmed by everything I needed to do. I didn't have a cleaner and used to get up on a Saturday morning and clean the loos, muttering to myself and growling at the family whenever they came near me. By nine o'clock

Saturday morning, all the children had seen was me being grumpy, and my husband would also be stressed out with everything I had flung at him. It was a bonkers decision driven by an intent to save money, but it resulted in a whole family being unhappy.

I soon admitted to myself that I couldn't cope. We were fortunately in a position where we were financially able to pay for help (although it was a struggle at the time). If you aren't able to afford professional help, then you will need to look to your partner (if you have one) and those around you.

Do I have to? How often have we heard that cry? In an ideal world, our children would help us with the basic chores around the home without a grumble. They would understand how they contribute to the running of the home so we wouldn't have to follow them around the house, picking up wet towels and coats. Sounds amazing, doesn't it? I don't know many people whose children are this good around the home, but there are things you can do to edge them into a better place.

Encourage your children to do more. Never give up when you've asked them to do something, even if you've asked ten times, otherwise you will teach them that if they ignore you for long enough, the problem will go away. Pay them to do jobs that you would pay others to do for you. I won't pay my children to empty the dishwasher, but I do if they clean the car.

Making sure your children help around the house is really important because not only does it help you, it also instils solid values in them as they grow.

Your partner won't help.   As we explored earlier in the book, women are still taking on greater responsibility for running the home, whether they are working or not. But it's important to look at what's driving this behaviour.

Lack of awareness: Think through whether your partner really understands how you feel. Is it lack of awareness driving their behaviour? You may have put across specific and individual requests over a period of time, but do they understand why you're asking and how they can take on more responsibilities around the home?

Take them out to dinner, or even just for a drink, so you have their full attention. Share your story – why your work is so important to you, how things have changed since the children have got a bit bigger, how it feels when you are full on at work and then take on all the responsibility at home, and how the two of you need to work together to make it all work.

Recognising their limits: Have you ever been hard at work in the evenings, getting ready for the next day, putting the children to bed and loading the dishwasher, only to discover your partner sitting watching TV? Rather than being disrespectful, they may just be recognising their limits and knowing that they need to stop and recharge their batteries for the next day.

In these situations, you may feel everything building up, and it all now falls on you and you alone to keep going and keep on top of it all. Actually, could you look to copy their lead rather than expect them to follow yours? Maybe learn from them rather than being frustrated. They may be absolutely correct on this one.

Again, communication is key. You need to take some time out to discuss how you can manage the work better so that you both get the balance you need.

Differing standards: How long does it take to clear the table for dinner in your house? In mine, it takes my husband about seven seconds and me about ten minutes. He merely moves everything from the table... to the hearth. Done. When I do it, I file as I go, return belongings to bedrooms, tidying everything away.

Has he done the task better than me? No, we have both achieved the objective, which was to be able to sit at the table for dinner. My preference is to take the opportunity to clear up as I do it, but it doesn't mean my way is the right way. It is just my way.

Your partner may not work to the standard you deem to be the right one, or complete the tasks as fully as you do, but as long as there aren't any black socks in a whites wash and it means you have less to do, does it honestly matter?

If their idea of 'done' is causing a genuine problem (such as creating more work for you), then agree with them how the activity should be tackled and when it's finished. If it isn't causing a problem, stop watching over their shoulder, commenting on how they are doing. They will end up feeling like you are criticising them if you do, and ultimately this will stop them even trying. Remember, your way isn't the right way; it's just your way.

Your behaviour: Reflect on whether your behaviours are driving your partner's actions. If they do an activity badly or ignore your request altogether, do you take over? You may do this because it's easier and quicker to do it yourself, but what is that telling them? It's a clear message that as long as they have the resilience to stick it out, you'll do it in the end.

You can't force them to change their behaviour, but you can change your own to influence theirs. Spend time sharing your aspirations and how they can help you. Learn how to improve your influencing skills and stop doing everything because it's easier or quicker. Agree what feels fair for them to take on. Expect some frustration, bargaining and anger as they move through the different stages we all experience as we go through change.[16]

---

16   The Change Curve model, Elisabeth Kübler-Ross

If you can't afford professional help, are a single parent, or your efforts to shift the balance of responsibility with your partner and children aren't making any difference, you will need to be even tougher on yourself when you are looking at the responsibilities you need to stop. Without the right level of support in the home, you are going to have to take much less on. This may feel aspirational, but you are in a position where you have a limited number of levers to flex. You aren't superwoman, so be realistic in terms of what you can take on.

MAKING IT WORK

Juliette, mother to Jack and Charlie, careers advisor

Juliette had always enjoyed her job as a careers advisor. She was good at it and loved helping others on their own professional journey.

When she had her two boys, she knew she wanted and needed to continue working, but she also knew that she and her husband would struggle if she was full time as he spent a lot of the week travelling around the country in his role as a sales manager. So, she reduced her hours to thirty each week, and every day worked from 9am until 3pm. When the boys were very young, it meant that they didn't have a long day at the childminder's, and when they went to school, it meant she could drop them off and pick them up during term time (they were with the childminder during the holidays).

Some ideas to try

- If someone offers help – take it.

- Recognise that taking your children to extra-curricular activities is a choice. You may want to expose them to new experiences, but remember that you can balance that out against clubs offered in school which don't make the same pull on you and your time.

- If your partner talks about 'babysitting' or 'helping you' around the house, call them out on it. It is their home as much as yours and the children are theirs too. You don't need help; you need a partnership.

- Keep talking to your partner. When you're both working and running a home, it's hard, but keeping your communication channels open will help you understand each other's needs and make sure you support each other properly.

- Encourage your children to do more around the house. Never give up asking them. If you do, it will teach them that if they ignore you for long enough, the request will go away. Create incentives to persuade them to help you or pay them to do jobs you would pay other people to do.

10
Skill Three – Manage The Day To Day

'Organising is what you do before you do something, so that when you do it, it is not all mixed up.'
— A. A. Milne

The number of tasks we have to manage on a daily basis can feel overwhelming and the idea of keeping everything under control is sometimes daunting.

It's hard. There's so much to do, from making the children's packed lunches to paying invoices at work to setting up a meeting with a new client. It feels never-ending. The problem is that when we become overwhelmed with day-to-day activities, we risk pushing everything else to one side – whether that's giving ourselves the time we need to focus on creating a fulfilling career, time with our children, or even just sitting having a coffee in a quiet house, not doing anything at all.

Being on top of your tasks is never going to make you feel fulfilled and contented; what's important is to manage your day to day, giving you the space you need to enjoy the rest of your life. However organised or unorganised you are comfortable being, it is important to minimise the amount of time you spend on your tasks, making sure you are working as efficiently as you can so you have more time for the other areas of your life.

There are some simple steps you can take to minimise the time you spend on daily 'stuff'.

Set yourself up for success

Step 1: Automate as much as you can. By removing as much of the thinking behind your day-to-day tasks as you can, you are freeing up time and headspace to focus on other areas of your life. You will need to invest some time initially, but you will quickly feel the benefit.

Set up direct debits or standing orders for all regular payments, from your TV licence to your credit card bill. Most of the main banks have easy-to-use websites and apps, and you can also use them to pay in cheques or transfer money to a friend, all from the comfort of your living room.

Set up recurring calendar events for everyone's birthdays and wedding anniversaries. If it's someone you need to send a card to or buy a gift for, add an email reminder to be sent to you the week before.

Design a daily checklist for what the children need to take to school – PE kit, recorder, homework etc. Stick it on the back of a door at their eye height, and if they are old enough, get them to take responsibility for packing their bags each morning.

Step 2: Find the right tool to help you. There are lots of different tools that can help you keep track of the day-to-day activities. Personally, I'm a huge fan of apps which I can access across all my devices. Wunderlist is fantastic if you like lists – there's nothing better than being able to tick something off when you've completed it. If you like to create a more visual picture of your tasks, check out Trello where you create a 'card' for each task and move it across the screen as you start and then finish it.

There are lots more out there so it's worth spending a little bit of time finding the right one for you. I suggest you use something specifically designed to help you with the day to day rather than your inbox. It's not designed to be a task repository, so it's difficult to keep it exclusively for tasks.

Once you've worked out what tool you are going to use, bring in all the tasks that you visualised in the first skill. You now have one place where you can keep your arms around everything.

Start finishing

Step 3: Be efficient. MRI scans show that when we attempt to do two things at once, our mind simply switches attention between the two; we cannot physically perform both at the same time. We have a frontal lobe which controls what we prioritise because our minds are unable to process two tasks at the same time.

We often talk about 'multitasking', but the word originates from the computer science world and refers to how machines operate. A computer's processor can switch back and forth between different tasks in a fraction of a second. The human brain takes up to fifteen minutes to fully focus on a task once we switch our attention to it. We actually context switch rather than multitask. This means that when we tackle a series of activities at the same time, it takes us longer to complete them than it would if we had attempted to do them consecutively because we have to consider the switching time involved every time we flip between each one.

Starting work makes us feel better, but we need to resist this natural urge of ours. We need to stop starting and start finishing.

We hear about the benefits of decluttering our lives on a physical level, but it's important to do so on an electronic level as well. If we use the analogy of an 85-page newspaper, it is estimated that we receive over 174 newspapers' worth of information every day compared to 40 pages back in 1986.[17] Our brains are constantly having to work out what is useful and necessary, and what isn't.

Unsubscribe from as many promotional emails as you can. For those that are left, set up a rule so that they are sent to a separate folder. You don't lose any of the emails and you can access them easily if you're out shopping, but you aren't having to process each one that comes into your inbox. Turn the alerts off on your phone for emails, news updates, social media updates – they break your concentration and distract you from the moment you are in.

Step 4: Keep chipping away. Success isn't about minimising the number of tasks you have still to do; as a working mother, you are always going to have lots to do. What's more important is making sure you have your arms around everything and that you finish every task just in time.

---

17   *The Telegraph*, 'Welcome to the information age – 174 newspapers a day'

Each morning, take a look at your tasks and make sure you know which need to be done that day. Add any new tasks in. From remembering to send in £1 for non-uniform day, to emails you've received about the next parents' evening, make sure you include everything in there.

Keep challenging yourself on whether everything you include is an activity that really needs to be done. Do you need to order all of your bank statements, credit card statements and other financial bills using a carefully designed filing system? Would it be easier to save the papers chronologically as they arrive in the post, and if you have to do a bit of searching at some point in the future to find a certain gas bill, then so be it? Always remember that good is good enough.

Then just keep working away. Make sure you're doing what you need to do to stay on top of the important things for that day, but not doing too much.

My daughter recently gave me a clear nudge when I was getting carried away with doing rather than enjoying life. Last year as we were approaching Christmas, she reminded me that it's not just about the logistics – the practicalities of buying the presents and sending the cards. I'd been so focused on all of the preparations, I had forgotten the most important thing about the festive season is spending time with my family.

Finally, when you finish something, enjoy ticking it off. There is something inherently satisfying about physically recognising you've completed a task, so savour the moment.

MAKING IT WORK

Jess, mother to Tom, stepmother to James, retail assistant

Jess finds that she is easily overwhelmed by the responsibilities she faces as a working mother. She knows that to stop herself feeling overwhelmed, she needs to make sure she isn't falling too far behind on her tasks during the week. She's created a routine whereby, during her morning commute on the train, she aims to complete one of her most important tasks. This is generally a phone-based activity such as replying to one of the boys' party invites or paying a bill. Although this activity in itself isn't enough to manage everything, it means she's completing one of her most important activities every day.

She also works to keep her inbox down to an absolute minimum where she has no more than twenty emails in there at any one time. And she has turned all notifications off on her phone for incoming emails, social media alerts, text messages, news updates, everything. This approach is personal to Jess and wouldn't work for everyone, but it helps her feel more in control, which is important to her.

Some ideas to try

- Do one thing at a time. Multitasking is the enemy of focus. Instead, focus on one activity and do it properly before moving on to the next one.

- Always be thinking of how people around you can help you more. My cleaner changes the sheets on my bed. She also washes them and hangs them out for me. My daughter writes our Christmas card envelopes and a friend pays her babysitter to wrap her Christmas presents for her.

- Plan your meals a week ahead rather than spending time each day thinking about what to eat and then shopping.

- Eat the frog. Mark Twain once said that if the first thing you do each morning is to eat a live frog, you can be comforted in knowing that it is probably the worst thing that is going to happen to you all day long. No matter how hard it is, tackle your biggest, most important task first – your 'frog'; the one you are most likely to procrastinate over. You'll feel better for it.

- Make sure you give yourself focus time and regular breaks. Look into the Pomodoro Technique which is a time-management method developed by Francesco Cirillo in the late 1980s. The idea is to create periods of focused time, traditionally twenty-five minutes in length, which are separated by short breaks.

11
Skill Four – Build Meaning Into Your Work

'If you're always trying to be normal you will never know how amazing you can be.'
— Maya Angelou

In Japanese culture, the reason for being is referred to as *ikigai*. The Japanese believe that discovering one's ikigai through one's passion, mission, profession and vocation brings satisfaction and meaning to life.

As mothers, we know our children give our lives meaning. As women with careers, we spend time away from our families. We want to make sure this time is full of meaning and purpose so that it feels worth it. If you work in a job you dislike, it's stressful; if you work in a job you love, it's a passion.

When we are engaged in meaningful work, our actions align with our core values and beliefs. We have a clear sense of purpose which feels incredibly fulfilling. We are motivated to put effort into our work, knowing that we will reap the rewards. We genuinely enjoy our work and can appreciate the richness it gives our lives beyond our family life.

Some working mothers struggle to find a career that gives them the meaning they need. Many feel they've never found it, lost it, or in some way they're falling short. They become bored, disillusioned with work, believe that being a working mother isn't for them, it's just not worth it. Being away from the family feels all the more difficult.

One of the most satisfying jobs I ever had was working in a chocolate shop in Sevenoaks after university. Before I joined, I never imagined I would find such purpose through working there. It wasn't intended as a first step in my career, but it taught me an awful lot in terms of customer service and running a small business. It was a place of great emotion and connection to the town through births, anniversaries, Valentine's Day, Easter. I heard so many personal stories, I felt part of the community, and I helped people to share a little joy with their loved ones. At that point in my life, it was exactly the right job to give me the meaning I needed.

People don't fall into meaningful work by accident or through good fortune. Nor do we find it from our external environment. Joining an organisation which is brilliant at creating engaging workplaces where each employee becomes part of nurturing an inclusive, cohesive and successful culture is a great start, but by itself isn't enough. It only creates an external environment that we enjoy. We find meaning in our lives from inside ourselves, and as individuals, we need to build this ourselves.

Be the real you at work

The first three steps to building meaning into your work are to know what motivates you, make genuine

117

friendships at work, and link your work to the greater good.

Step 1: Know what motivates you. Humans are motivated both intrinsically and extrinsically. Intrinsic motivators come from within us – we are interested and find enjoyment in the task itself. It may help us learn, give us a sense of purpose, be an opportunity for self-expression, or we simply have fun when we are doing it. Extrinsic motivators are rewards external to ourselves and the event. We are driven by the outcome of the event, such as a pay rise, promotion, praise or fear of punishment.

We need a mixture of both intrinsic and extrinsic motivators in our work to fully satisfy our psychological needs. People who focus on their extrinsic motivators can be incredibly well paid, have the job title they've always dreamt of, enjoy a huge bonus every year, yet feel empty. Being engaged in work that we don't find motivating is unfulfilling and dissatisfying.

I know I'm most motivated intrinsically when I'm in an environment where I am stretched intellectually, working on interesting projects and part of a fun team. From an extrinsic motivation perspective, it's as simple as bringing in the money I need to support my family.

I once worked with someone who had a picture of a yacht pinned up by his desk. The picture served as a reminder as to why he was working. He was only a few years off retirement, had no children and had already paid off his mortgage. Earning the money to buy a yacht was what motivated him in his work.

Spend time thinking through what motivates you intrinsically and extrinsically. If you are intrinsically motivated by the social aspect of work – meeting new people, for example – make sure you build the opportunity for this into your day. Perhaps volunteer to mentor someone or organise the social get-togethers. If you are highly extrinsically motivated, then develop a plan to deliver your objectives and secure your bonus or end up with the great job title you've always wanted. Whatever it is, make sure that you are spending the time and effort on what motivates you at work.

Step 2: Make genuine friendships at work. We share our professional successes and go through tough times with our co-workers. When one or more of the people we work with are good friends rather than just work colleagues, we are happier and less stressed. We are seven times more engaged in our jobs,[18] we feel connected to the company and we believe that our roles are important.

Seek out people that you feel a natural connection with; people who have similar values to you. Then invest time in building positive relationships.

18 Gallup engagement survey

Schedule in time to go for lunch or coffee, or make a point of casually popping round to their desk for a chat. Maybe take a junior person in your team under your wing or take the lead in setting up your team charity day. All of these will drive genuine and warm relationships with those you work with and ultimately help you to build meaning into your work.

Step 3: Link your work to the greater good. Purpose can be found in almost all roles when we appreciate the bigger picture – the ultimate purpose of our individual roles. Playgroup helpers provide children with the first critical step in their education, so they can see how they are helping to positively shape the children's lives. Independent bookkeepers reconciling expenses are helping entrepreneurs to run successful businesses. Cleaners in a hospital manage the basic domestic chores, but are really making sure they minimise the risk of germs and infection, and maximise the patients' chances of recovery.

My husband worked as an environmental manager for a local council many years ago. He found such meaning in his work as he was serving the community, making it a better place for people to live and work. He's now working as a business manager in an inner-London school, helping young people to get the best possible start in life. He's always worked really hard to build meaning into his work, and as a result, he finds it hugely rewarding and satisfying.

Today I have tried my best

There are three further steps to take which help you to do your best, every day.

Step 4: Set clear goals for yourself. If you're anything like me, you groan when someone asks you where you want to be in five years' time. And there's certainly something to be said for grabbing opportunities as they arise rather than having everything planned out to the nth degree. At the same time, a clear vision of the future prevents us stumbling through life, taking a chance that it will work out OK. Goals keep us focused and prevent us being distracted by the mass of other things we have going on in our lives.

People tend to answer the question 'Where do you want to be in a few years' time?' in a tangible way. It may be related to a promotion or reaching a certain grade, perhaps setting up a business or reinventing a career. That's great if you have this clarity, but many of us don't.

I have always been one who searches out opportunities, and if I feel they are going to take me on an interesting journey, I grab them with both hands. A while back, when I was a permanent employee, this didn't sit well in end-of-year performance conversations, particularly when I was working in a commercial team and everyone around me was highly motivated by extrinsic drivers: promotions, job titles and recognised status or hierarchy. It isn't that extrinsic motivators aren't important to me; they are, but I need a balance between those and the intrinsic ones that often drive my career decisions. For me, it's around enjoying the work I do and learning as well as earning enough money to give my family the lifestyle I want to.

If you have a long-term vision, that's fantastic. Hold on to it. Beneath your vision, set the goals that you need to achieve towards that vision. If you are someone without a long-term strategy, it's OK. Just set yourself goals that keep you focused on developing and learning rather than getting lost in the day-to-day activities of your job.

Each year, I set myself two or three goals. This year, they are launching this book and taking more time off in school holidays. The second one may seem slightly strange to some of you, but if I set it as a goal, it is front of mind and I'm much more likely to do it.

Step 5: Be fully engaged.   You're busy; there's a piece of work you have to finish before you can go home and see your kids. You tear yourself away to go to a meeting. It's a bit tedious and all you want to do is get out of there as quickly as you can.

How do you think your behaviour comes across during the meeting? Others around you can tell when you're not fully engaged; they will pick it up from your body language, your tone of voice, how much you talk and what you say.

Engagement is intrinsic and individual. It's when we are connected to a business and its purpose. It's a voluntary action – no one can force us to become engaged.

If you'd been fully engaged at the meeting, would you have entered the room with a more positive mindset, asked more questions and created interesting conversations? Would you have been able to lift the meeting (if you were finding it dull, the chances are others were too) and ultimately influence its outcome?

Each hour that passes is an hour that we will never get back again, so we need to do our best to make the most of each and every one of them. If we don't and we are miserable, it's our own misery, not our employer's, our boss's or our co-workers', so it's only we who lose out.

When someone asks for your time or engagement in an activity, firstly, make sure you only say yes if it is the right thing for you or the organisation. If you say yes, fully commit yourself. That means no checking your phone while other people are talking, tapping away on your laptop or thinking about how to approach your next project. Those around you will feel respected and valued if you give them your full attention, and you will walk out knowing you've done your best.

Step 6: Remember why you work. Most of us don't have the luxury of working solely for pleasure. We work to bring money into the household, so ultimately our efforts are an act of service to those we love. We work hard to provide a certain standard of living for our children, perhaps so that we are able to take them on holidays that expose them to wonderful life experiences or to provide a positive role model for them.

No working mother ever has only their own needs in mind as they work. We work for those we care about and that thought keeps us going through the good times and the bad. When you've had a success at work, good feedback from a client, a promotion or finished a big piece of work that you're proud of, share it with your family. Tell them over dinner what you did and why it means so much to you, go out for some family time or buy a bottle of fizz to share with your partner.

Every day, ask yourself, 'Have I tried my best to build meaning into my work?'

MAKING IT WORK

Lucy, mother to Arwen and Rhys, art curator

Many women like to separate their work and their home life as much as they can. Lucy does the opposite and actively involves her children in her work. Lucy's children go along to her exhibitions and art installations; they have an understanding and appreciation of her work, and of art and design, in a way they wouldn't otherwise. She believes that when they see her work hard, and how passionate she is about her job, it helps them to build their own strong work ethic.

Being a positive role model for both her son and her daughter is important to Lucy, and she encourages them to work hard at school and aspire to having a career they love. She is particularly aware of showing her daughter how she can successfully combine motherhood and her career as she grows up.

Some ideas to try

- Set yourself between three and five goals (depending on the size) for the year, both professional and personal. Be realistic in what you can achieve; being successful will increase your sense of satisfaction, whereas failing to deliver on all of them will make you feel low.

- Create visual reminders of your vision (if you have one) and your goals and stick them up in your workplace or around your desk so you can see what you are working towards.

- Even though you are stretched from a time perspective, carve out time for creating strong, trusted and genuine relationships at work.

- Leave your laptop and phone behind when you go into a workshop or meeting.

- Celebrate your professional successes with your family.

12

SKILL FIVE – DEVELOP STRONG ROUTINES

'A body without bones would be a limp impossible mess, so a day without steady routine would be disruptive and chaotic.'
— May Sarton

Much of our time with our children follows a similar pattern each day. They get up at the same time for school each morning, sit down to do homework after school, eat dinner at a similar time each evening, and go to bed at roughly the same time each night. The predictability of their routines instils a sense of calm; they know what to expect and it minimises stress.

As adults, we often fail to create routines aimed at benefiting ourselves as well as our children. As a result, we can feel like we are overwhelmed with the stress of last-minute thinking – from what to wear to which big items need to be completed at work that day, to what's for dinner that evening.

How strong routines help us

I used to view having a routine as being boring, rigid and constraining. I would pride myself on getting from the bed to the office in the shortest amount of time possible, having crammed in as much as I could without a thought for whether I was setting myself up for a successful and productive day. On some days, I would have helped two small children out of the house with all the kit, attended two doctors' appointments (one for each of them), written a list of ingredients we needed for dinner and speed read my book-club book for a meet that evening. On a task level, I was rocking it, but I felt totally frazzled before my workday had even begun.

Carefully developed routines create a logical sequence to our activities and a framework to operate under. We know what comes next, what we are doing ahead of time without much thought, so there is no last-minute planning, prioritising and making decisions as we go or rushing from one thing to the next. With a routine, there is less room for forgetfulness. We can prioritise what is most important to us, incorporate these activities into our routine and make sure they are done first and out of the way. We don't need to rely on determination and willpower to tackle our least favourite tasks and it lessens the chances of us procrastinating over them.

There's a flow to our day – activities seamlessly move from one into another. Our thinking time is reduced so we become more efficient and calmer. Ultimately strong routines help us to operate at our peak performance levels each day.

Create a routine that works for you

If you're an early bird, you will be most effective before lunchtime, whereas night owls will find their creative energy late in the day. Be mindful of this as you design your routine. Where possible, match the activities with the right time of day for you.

Mornings for working mothers are often simply about getting out of the door in one piece and managing not to forget anything. Irrespective of whether you are an early bird or a night owl, try to balance out this time between essential tasks with a bit of you time. Pack lunches and gym kits, but also leave enough time to focus on yourself so you feel calm and ready for the day ahead.

On a great day, my morning routine includes a few minutes of calm before I get out of bed to prioritise my activities for the day, yoga, a cup of my favourite coffee and having time to dress and put on my make-up. In reality, I rarely manage all of these – I get frantic pleading phone calls from my daughter at 8am every so often when she has forgotten her flute or homework and I end up dashing out of the door to take them to her at school. On those days, I am back to being lucky if I have time to brush my hair. No clean shirts, a high temperature, a lost left shoe – all these things can easily derail a morning routine. But during those moments, I remember that by at least aiming for a good morning routine, I stand a chance of achieving it.

Our energy levels are often dropping by midday and the pressures of work can derail our determination to create the time to tick a couple of things off our to-do list. But try to take a good few minutes to have some lunch away from your desk, giving yourself a mental break and the opportunity to tackle a couple of easy admin tasks. I deliberately buy lunch outside the office so that I have to leave my desk. Even if I eat on the way back to my office, it gives me a few minutes' quiet or the opportunity for a quick phone call to catch up with my husband.

Use evenings to prepare for the next day as much as possible. Pack bags – encourage your children to do this if they are old enough. Think about what you are going to wear – I have a horrible tendency to have a mind blank in the mornings and just stare into my wardrobe minute after minute if I don't plan.

When I'm at home, I have a routine I follow to set me up as well as possible, physically and mentally, for the next day. I'll try to eat before 7pm to allow my body to fully digest my meal before I go to bed. I'll always have a hot shower. (Hot water encourages blood to move to the surface of the skin. When you get out of the shower, the dilated blood vessels radiate out the heat and your core body temperature falls, which helps you to fall asleep more quickly and, in many adults, induces deeper sleep.)[19] And finally, I'll read for a bit before switching the light off.

Ideally, you want to give yourself at least eight hours of 'sleep opportunity', which is the time that you are trying to sleep during the night. Sometimes this is impossible, particularly with younger children if they aren't sleeping through the night or with older ones who need collecting from clubs and social events, but it's important to try. Sleep is critical to our long-term physical and mental health as well as how we feel the next day.

I have never slept well and this drives my commitment to a healthy bedtime routine. The brain associates sound and smell strongly with experiences, so in the past, I've used this to let my brain know that it's time

19 Walker, Matthew (2018) Why We Sleep: The New Science of Sleep and Dreams. Penguin Books Ltd.

for sleep. I played the same sound of waves crashing on a beach to myself each evening – some people play a piece of music they love – and warmed lavender oil in my bedroom. It's also a great time of day to meditate if you can squeeze it in.

Remember that 'the best-laid plans of mice and men often go awry' (translated from the Robert Burns poem 'To A Mouse'). Routines are great, but it's important not to be ruled by them, and if something comes up which takes priority, be able to flex and adapt around it.

Finally, create your own 'not-to-do' list. As important as strong positive routines are, you need to understand what you definitely don't want to be doing as part of your day. A not-to-do list helps you see what you need to focus on to protect yourself.

My own not-to-do list includes:

- Don't check work emails before I officially start work for the day
- Don't allow work notifications on my phone (neither email nor WhatsApp, nor any other app)
- Don't overdo my time on social media (I control my time on social media as much as my children's)
- Don't attend more than one evening networking event each week

I try to stick to my list, but don't always manage to. Remember that good is good enough; don't worry about creating the perfect routine. You need one that feels about right, so try it out and learn from what doesn't work for you.

MAKING IT WORK

Katie, mother to Eva, HR advisor

Katie works part time as an HR advisor and used to use her train commute to check her work emails. As soon as she got on to the train in the morning, she opened up the app on her phone and started working through all the emails that had arrived in her inbox. Her theory was that by the time she reached her desk, she would have caught up with anything that had happened while she wasn't working.

In reality, her stress level would rocket as soon as she started reading the emails. Being on her phone on the train rather than in the office, she was rarely able to actually do anything about the emails; she was just passively absorbing the urgent requests and increasing her stress levels enormously. It was a horrible feeling, and she eventually realised that she needed to stop herself looking at them until she arrived at her desk. By doing this, she completely removed her stress and suffered none of the consequences she had imagined. After leaving the office, she now stops working at the station stop exactly half way between work and her home to give her time to switch off before she walks in the door.

Some ideas to try

- Go to bed early enough to give yourself eight hours' 'sleep opportunity'.

- Even if you feel you can cope comfortably on seven hours' sleep or fewer, this is just because your brain and body have become used to it. Research shows that not sleeping for eight hours has a detrimental effect on our body and mind – our ability to learn and retain is impaired, our risk of cancer and Alzheimer's is increased, and our metabolism is lowered to name but a few. The sleep also needs to be regular. There is no such thing as making up for sleep at the weekends; once the night's sleep has gone, it's gone.

- Create a not-to-do list and stick to it whenever you can.

- Build exercise into your daily routine. Exercise keeps your weight down, reduces stress, your risk of cancer, diabetes and heart disease, and benefits your mental health.

- Switch off screens two hours before bedtime – blue light disrupts your circadian rhythm (your sleeping and waking cycle).

- You don't need to overthink your routines; they are merely a conscious choice to live your life in a certain way through healthy repetition.

PART FOUR

NOW THAT YOU DON'T HAVE TO BE PERFECT, YOU CAN BE GOOD

13
Becoming Proficient

'How wonderful it is that nobody need wait a single moment before starting to improve the world.'
— Anne Frank

You are now equipped with the principles and skills every working mother needs to become contented. The trick is to gently build up your competence levels against every principle and skill in parallel rather than focusing on each in turn, trying to excel. Work on improving your proficiency and fully embed each one in your life through practice, creating habits and making sure that you are delegating effectively.

Keep practising. Make mistakes and learn from them. Successful people do the same things over and over again. An artist paints picture after picture before their final masterpiece; an athlete practises daily, fine-tuning their techniques to improve their performance. As you practise the principles and skills, you too will become more comfortable and accomplished.

Creating habits

The key, as you practise the principles and skills, is to turn them into habits. As you repeat them, you will move from a state of consciously competent to unconsciously competent, and ultimately your actions will become subconscious. The principles and skills will have become habits.

Humans are creatures of habit. Just like our children, we adults relish the familiarity of them. They need less willpower to tackle than a new skill – brushing our teeth in the morning doesn't require determination or willpower because it's simply part of our routine. Habits also reduce procrastination and the thinking time involved in certain tasks. We don't question or challenge what we are doing; we just get on with it, accepting it's what we do.

You can accelerate creating habits out of everything you have learned through following some simple steps.

Step 1: Gradually build up. As you build up your habits, make sure each one starts off easy enough for you to encompass the change into your life without it feeling like just another thing to do. For example, rather than starting with thirty minutes of meditation a day, start with five minutes, or go for a run once a week and build up rather than aiming for something that frankly feels unachievable right now. You will then be successful from the start and your motivation will increase, which in turn will make it easier to stick to the habit. Be consistent and gradually build it up.

Step 2: Anchor the new habit to an established one. I've always enjoyed my morning espresso, it's a real treat for me, so when I began to build yoga into my morning routine, I attached it to my love of my coffee, thereby creating a positive association. After I have made my morning coffee and enjoyed the aromas permeating my home, I set it beside me while I do my yoga.

Step 3: Give yourself time to embed the habit. There are varying thoughts in terms of how long it takes to build a habit, but in truth it depends on the habit itself and how you personally respond to it. You will find some of the habits you take on are easy to build, while others require more effort.

Commit to a minimum time you will give your habit to bed in. I always recommend one month. During this period, create a routine so that you practise the habit at the same time each day. For example, you could build yoga into your morning routine and keep doing it. Repeat it until it becomes part of what you do and who you are.

Step 4: Celebrate your achievements. Celebrate and focus on progress, not perfection. Say to yourself, 'I am a work in progress and that's OK.' Create a reward for yourself to enjoy when you've completed a certain number of days of the habit. It could be a movie night with your partner or carving out time to do something you love.

Step 5: Accept and plan for the stumbles. If you get off track, simply get back on track as quickly as you can. We all make mistakes and encounter obstacles to our progress. It could be time pressures, an unexpected pick up from school or a child being ill. If you prepare for these, they won't trip you up when they do come.

Create a Plan B around your new habits. Tell yourself, 'If I don't find time for my personal project at the end of the day, I will get up thirty minutes earlier the next day,' or, 'If it's raining and I can't go for a run, I will work out at the gym instead.'

How to delegate effectively in the home

In Chapter 9 we addressed how to do less and the importance of delegating wherever you can. Delegating in itself is a skill. Whether you are delegating to your partner, someone else in the family or paying a professional, it's important you make sure they have everything they need to be successful, and then let go.

Step 1: Find the right person. Finding the right person to help you is critical. If that's your partner, great; if you are looking for professional support, invest time making sure you find the right person for you. When you bring in the best person, you will be able to fully delegate and step back. The wrong one will just take up more of your precious time.

I had a cleaner for a while who was lovely, but she kept breaking things: cupboard doors that literally took us hours to mend, ornaments and the vacuum cleaner. The third time she broke the vacuum cleaner, it wasn't repairable. I had to face the fact that she wasn't taking the worry and thinking time away from the housework, and her working for me wasn't sustainable. I felt terrible, but it had reached the stage where I had to let her go.

Step 2: Make sure they are set up for success. Obviously, if you are paying for professional help, you can expect this stage to be quite short as they will already be experts in their field. It is just a matter of familiarising them with your own specific situation and needs, and then they should be ready to go. If they aren't, question whether you have the right person in place. If you find you are continually needing to invest a lot of time and energy coaching or supporting someone professionally to do the job you are paying them to do, then they aren't the right person to help you.

When you are looking to delegate to your partner or someone on a personal level, firstly, make sure the request is fair and your expectations are realistic. If it's a new activity that they haven't done before, they will probably need clear guidance from you when they begin. As they become more used to the task and build their confidence, you can step back.

Step 3: Let go. Once you have found the right person and they have developed the capability or skills they need to take on the responsibility without your support, you can fully step back. When you step back, you are showing them you trust them and they will feel empowered. This may all sound like overkill if you are thinking about something basic like keeping the kitchen clean and tidy, but often your responsibilities are much more complex than you may think. Remember they may only feel simple to you because you are so used to doing them.

Once you think you've let go, if you find yourself still thinking about the responsibility and closely watching what's happening, this is false delegation. Push away thoughts that no one else can do the activity as well as you. What's important is that someone is taking away some of the load from you and helping you to create space in your life. Unless you properly step back, you aren't embracing this opportunity.

Be patient. Delegating responsibilities you have been doing for years will take time. At the beginning it will feel like it's taking you more time than it would to just do it yourself, but persevere. Once you start doing less, you will be able to breathe a little more easily. You will have freed up time and energy.

Time for a change?

If you aren't finding the meaning in your work that you want and need, it may be time to consider a change. But change can be really scary, and sometimes it feels easier to put up with what you have today – better the devil you know.

Humans have a natural tendency to avoid losses rather than focusing on acquiring equivalent gains (loss aversion).[20] Some studies show that losses are almost twice as psychologically powerful as gains. We don't want to feel the loss of what we have already secured, be it money, emotions, relationships, status. This means that we will often put up with something, even when the alternative would be preferable. Change can be an uncomfortable process. As a result, we sometimes avoid pursuing the type of work we really want to do and instead choose the safe path, even if it's far less satisfying.

---

20 Loss aversion – one of the cognitive biases where cognitive biases are systematic patterns of deviation from norm or rationality in judgment

There are five main stages we all experience as we go through change: denial, anger, depression, bargaining and acceptance. Being aware and accepting that we go through each of these stages helps us navigate an easier path through them during changes in our lives.

Use some simple coaching questions to help you understand yourself and your needs better and establish whether you need to be considering a change.

- What are my core values?

- What motivates me?

- When I imagine being in a great job in twelve months' time, what do I see, feel and hear?

- What are my natural talents?

- What would I do if I knew I couldn't fail?

- If I knew I only had five years left to live, what would I do differently?

The last question isn't intended to be terribly dramatic; it's included to help you imagine what kind of work you would want to do if you didn't have any of your current pressures.

Taking the decision to change jobs or the direction of your career can feel enormous. When I left the relative safety of a permanent job to set myself up as an independent consultant, I had to consider the loss of all the benefits that a permanent job brings:

my company pension, medical and life insurance, company car, a structured career path and the sense of belonging from working in a team. I wouldn't know what I was doing more than two or three months ahead, and that would mean bringing an instability into our home and family which was hard for both my husband and I to get our heads around.

My new path ahead was undeniably going to be challenging, but I was desperately unhappy and I knew it was having a terrible effect on my family. It was time to put the stress down and make some changes in my life.

I took a series of steps to make sure I was as well equipped to make the decision and take the leap as I could possibly be. I reflected on what motivated me in life and in my career using the coaching questions I listed earlier. Once I was sure that this new direction in my professional journey was right for me, I tested my likelihood of success in my new world by seeking advice from professionals and friends alike. Only then did I write my resignation letter.

I still, to this day, remember the terror I felt before I handed that letter over. Leaving a company where I had worked for fifteen years without a new job to go to was one of the hardest things I have ever done in my life. But I've never looked back. It was definitely time for me to change.

If you think you may be at that point in your life, consider your options really carefully, work through what motivates you, plan, and then... leap. The beauty of the decisions we make is that once we've made them, we then work hard to ensure they are the right ones. It's all up to you.

14

That's What Little Girls Are Made Of

'The future depends entirely on what each of us
does every day; a movement is only people moving.'
— Gloria Steinem

None of the principles and skills you have learned are complex. In fact, there is beauty in the simplicity of them. You know how to become a contented mother; you know the rules of the game.

The working mother principles and skills – a reminder

Know that good is good enough – being a great working mother isn't about perfection; it's knowing the standard you need to work to and then keeping to it.

Live in the moment – life is short, appreciate every day.

Be your own best friend – treat yourself with the same kindness you would a good friend.

Be resilient every day – be ready to cope with life's inevitable twists and turns.

Believe in yourself – have confidence that you have the skills you need to be the person you want to be.

Make everything visible – when you can see everything you need to do, you are able to prioritise easily and work through it effectively.

Do less – it's important to stop the non-essential activities and make sure you aren't taking on more and more.

Manage the day to day – use great techniques to manage all the work.

Build meaning into your work – you need to create meaning in your work yourself. It isn't something you find accidentally.

Develop strong routines – carefully developed routines instil a sense of calm and help you to protect your time and headspace.

Together we can shape the world

The world around us and the way we work are changing thanks to the shifting demographics of workers, technology, the economy and politics. The one model we have been offered for decades, where everyone works for one company, year after year, five days a week, is becoming outdated.

Baby boomers are retiring and this is creating talent shortages. Three different groups can fill this gap: the baby boomers themselves, millennials and working mothers. The practical challenge for businesses is that none of these groups want to work in line with the model we traditionally see; they want to engage with businesses differently, enjoy a more entrepreneurial environment, have more freedom to operate, experience less control. Working mothers (along with millennials) aren't hell bent on progressing up a career ladder; they want journeys, experiences and flexibility. To increase the talent pool, organisations will have to become more attractive to working mothers, millennials and retired baby boomers.

Technological advances in artificial intelligence and robots are driving automation of jobs, changing the skills we need in the workplace and the nature of work itself. New jobs will be created that we haven't even dreamt of yet and we will need different skills to undertake these roles. Humans will provide technological expertise, social and

149

emotional capabilities that machines aren't capable of. Although it can sometimes raise difficult questions, this disruption creates an opportunity for working mothers.

We often hear how women bring a different quality to leadership positions. A *Harvard Business Review* report confirmed that women are rated more highly than men in twelve of the sixteen competencies that go into outstanding leadership,[21] including the more nurturing competencies such as developing others and building relationships. They also excel in competencies such as establishing stretch goals and driving for results.

Organisations of the future need skills that women possess. Skill shortages are driving them to change from the traditional model. Both of these factors will affect working environments and result in them becoming more and more suited to working mothers.

We are all role models

Wolves were reintroduced into Yellowstone Park in 1995 after an absence of seventy years. With no active predators, the number of deer in the park had built up. As soon as the wolves arrived, they had an amazing effect. They killed deer which allowed new vegetation

---

21 'Are Women Better Leaders than Men?' Jack Zenger and Joseph Folkman, Harvard Business Review, 2012

growth. They also changed the behaviour of the deer, who started to avoid certain areas of the park. As a result, birds moved back into the park. Badgers, bears, mice, hawks and other animals started to thrive again. Forests grew and this stabilised the banks of the rivers, meaning that they meandered less. Although small in number, the wolves changed the ecosystem and physical geography of the park. Ultimately, they changed rivers.

Working mothers forging successful journeys for themselves in the workplace influence the way professions and industries operate and, ultimately, the world around us. Each and every one of us is a role model, but how many of us underestimate the effect we have? And how many of us are completely comfortable calling ourselves role models?

Resist building the idea of being a role model into something bigger than it is or needs to be. If you do, you risk giving yourself an excuse not to expect it every day from yourself and others. Bring it all back to basics; don't be afraid of being different, of standing out. Be proud, true to yourself, humble, and show others that it's OK to make mistakes.

Don't pretend to the outside world that your life is all manageable. When you do this, you are creating a perception that it is possible to have it all, and those around you will think they need to live up to a standard that actually isn't realistic. Instead, smile and admit that you and your life aren't perfect, but you are contented. Sometimes being contented means being a little messy and emotional, and that's OK.

When my daughter was three years old, a friend who didn't work came over for coffee with her son, who was in my daughter's nursery class. I went upstairs to check the children were OK and heard a terribly earnest conversation going on. My daughter was getting ready to go out to work as part of their mummies and daddies role-play game.

'But mummies don't work,' said my friend's son incredulously.

'Yes, they do,' retorted my daughter, even more incredulously. I felt so proud of her for her insistence and of myself as her role model.

Mummies do work. And they make a damn good job of it.

Have You Discovered?

One of the great joys in life for me is discovering material that gives me a new perspective on my life and ideas to try out. Here are a few of my favourite resources, all related in some way to *In This Moment*, that you may enjoy.

Looking after yourself:

Walker, M. (2018) Why We Sleep: The new science of sleep and dreams. New York: Penguin Books Ltd. (Available on audio)

Kristin Neff on self-compassion: https://self-compassion.org

Headspace app for meditation: www.headspace.com

Being the best you:

Amy Cuddy TED talk 'Fake It 'Til You Make It' (2012) www.youtube.com/watch?v=RVmMeMcGc0Y

Alan Watts 'Life Is Music': www.youtube.com/watch?v=tJNKs9hmmlE

When you want to change:

Heath, C. and D. (2010) *Switch: How to change things when change is hard.* New York: Random House Business. (Available on audio)

Pink, D. (2011) *Drive: The surprising truth about what motivates us.* Edinburgh: Canongate Books Ltd. (There is a fantastic ten-minute online animation summarising the key principles in the book.)

Know that it's the little things make a difference:

Drew Dudley TEDx talk *'Everyday Leadership' (2010)*, www.ted.com/talks/drew_dudley_everyday_leadership?language=en#t-70116

Chris Agnos talk *'How Wolves Change Rivers'*, https://chrisagnos.com/how-wolves-change-rivers

ACKNOWLEDGEMENTS

Thank you firstly to my husband for always supporting me in my professional journey, whatever direction I've decided to take. He is a true partner in the running of our home who has made endless Sunday roasts, run the children to activities and kept pushing me onwards while I have been writing this book.

I was fortunate to grow up with a family who always firmly believed that I could achieve everything I wanted to in life. You have all influenced my life enormously. Thank you to my parents and sister for all your love and understanding.

And, of course, thank you to my children. You are my inspiration and you fill me with love and joy every single day.

There would be no book without my working mother friends. Thank you for the laughter, the shoulders to cry on (literally sometimes), and for being so completely inspirational. You are all amazing.

Thank you to the team at S&S – The Change Society, especially to Pat and Adrian for their unwavering support and encouragement throughout the process of writing this book. It really did keep me going through the tough parts.

Finally, thank you to everyone who read the manuscript, challenged and advised me. You all helped to shape the book more than you could ever imagine.

The Author

Jacqueline Shakespeare is a contented working mother. She lives in London with her husband John and their two children. She loves being *in this moment* with her family, evenings out with friends, and those occasional moments of 'me time', losing herself in a book or photography. Like many working mothers, she has some days which are great, others she just about makes it through, and the odd one where she's found with a glass of Chianti in her hand, trying to work out where it all went wrong, determined to pick herself back up and face the next day afresh.

She also loves her work, and uses her own story and life experiences to inspire other working mothers to strive for, and achieve, contentment in their lives. She passionately believes that mothers can enjoy fulfilling careers without compromising other areas of their lives.

Jacqueline is an operating partner at S&S – The Change Society, helping clients solve complex business problems. She specialises in leading strategy development and helping organisations become 'change ready'.

An executive coach and speaker, she is passionate about the people and culture side of change, focusing on collaborative working, engagement and developing a growth mindset with clients.

Jacqueline is the author of *In This Moment* and co-author of *Pivot: Real Cut Through Stories by Experts at the Frontline of Agility and Transformation.*

You can contact Jacqueline at:

LinkedIn: Jacqueline Shakespeare

Email: jacqueline.shakespeare@ellisblue.co.uk

Lightning Source UK Ltd.
Milton Keynes UK
UKHW020958110719
345974UK00005B/223/P